More Windows to the World

Written and Illustrated
by
Nancy Everix

Cover by Vanessa Filkins

Copyright © Good Apple, Inc., 1985

ISBN No. 0-86653-316-8

Printing No. 987654321

GOOD APPLE, INC.
BOX 299
CARTHAGE, IL 62321-0299

W9-ABY-696

Dedicated to my family and
friends who gave their ideas,
support and encouragement.

Table of Contents

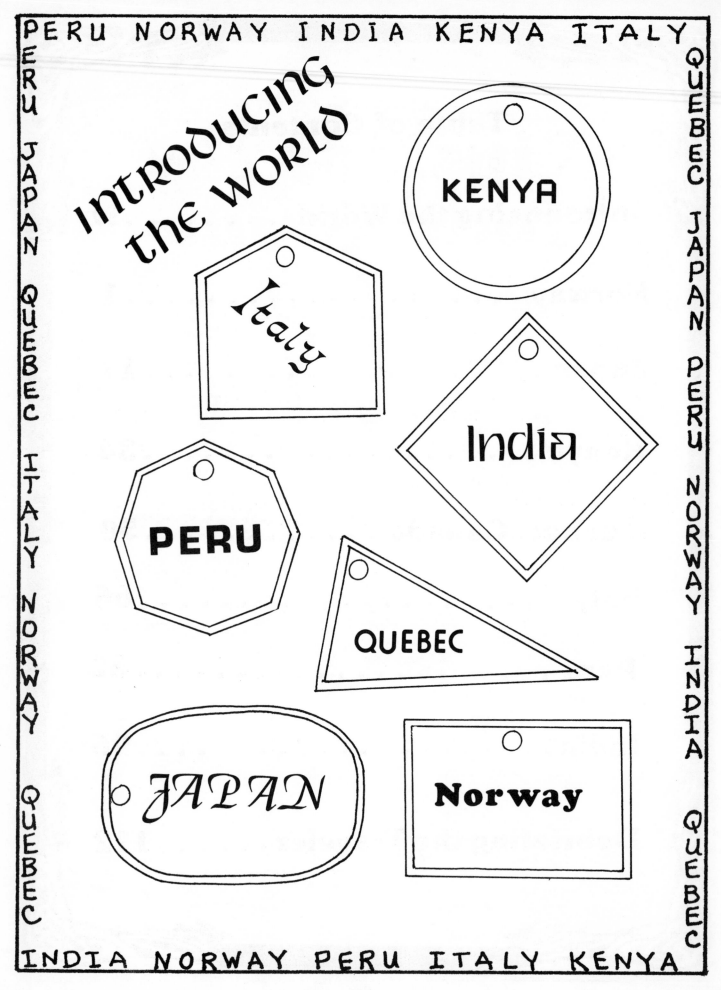

Tips for the Tour Guide

A year of travel sounds exciting, doesn't it? Your students will find your study of other cultures exciting and rewarding, also.

Use the backpack theme to develop "containers" for their work. Use the ideas in the next few pages to introduce the entire year's work. Design a banner or bumper sticker for each country as you study it. Large, colorful posters drawn by the students can also add excitement to your classroom. Additional firsthand experience can be gained by having the students request pen pals from another country. Often these contacts last a lifetime and the pen pals have the opportunity to meet each other. The following address is a clearing house for 40,000 young people ages 12-20 in the United States and 150 foreign countries and territories. Charges are $2.00 for individuals, but they do offer group rates.

WORLD PEN PALS
1690 Como Avenue
St. Paul, MN 55108

You may want to write to the international tourist offices to ask for free or inexpensive materials, posters and other visuals. You will have the best results when requesting materials if you use school letterhead stationery. A sample letter follows:

Dear Sirs:

Our school will be studying about your country in the next few weeks. We are interested in _____. We would appreciate any free or inexpensive materials, such as posters, brochures, films, etc., that you have available. These materials would enhance our students' appreciation of your country. If class-size orders are available, I would appreciate _____ copies.

Thank you for this valuable service to our children and our school.

Sincerely,
Teacher/Grade Level

These are the addresses:

JAPAN Trade Center
230 North Michigan
Chicago, IL 60601
Tel. 312-726-4390

QUEBEC Government Office
35 East Wacker Drive
Chicago, IL 60601
Tel. 312-726-0681

ITALIAN Government Travel Office
500 North Michigan
Chicago, IL 60611
Tel. 312-644-0990

NORWEGIAN Consulate General Office
360 North Michigan
Chicago, IL 60601
Tel. 312-782-7750

KENYA Tourist Office
60 East 56th Street
New York, NY 10022
Tel. 212-486-1300

INDIA Government Tourist Office
230 North Michigan
Chicago, IL 60601
Tel. 312-236-6899

PERUVIAN Tourist Information Center
366 Madison Avenue
New York, NY 10017
Tel. 212-883-0444

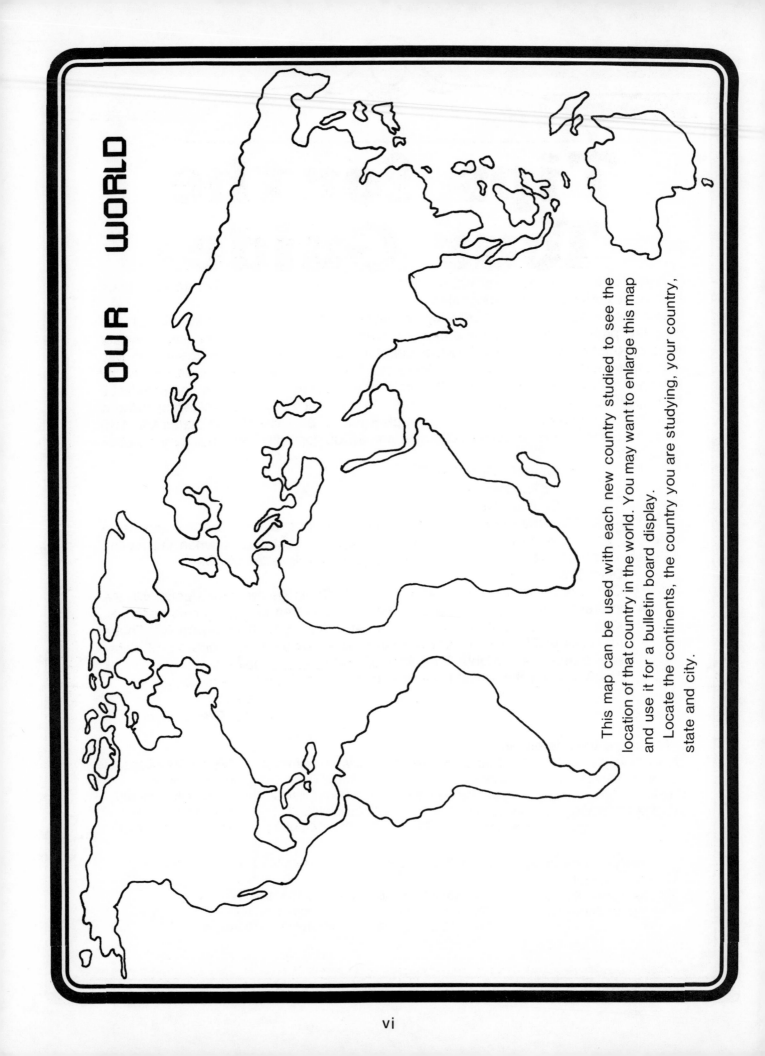

OUR WORLD

This map can be used with each new country studied to see the location of that country in the world. You may want to enlarge this map and use it for a bulletin board display.

Locate the continents, the country you are studying, your country, state and city.

DESIGN A  BACKPACK

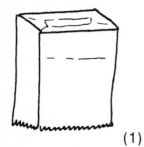

(1)

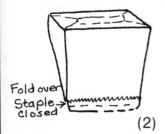

Fold over
Staple
closed →

(2)

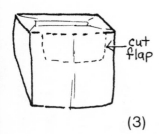

cut
flap ←

(3)

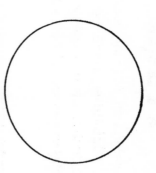

Design a shopping bag backpack for your worldwide travels.

Need: 1 large grocery bag (1)
Construction paper
Bright colored strips of cloth
(2" x 24")
2 brass fasteners

Directions: Fold over bag opening and staple closed.(2) Cut flap on the side of the bag that has no advertising.(3) Add 2 brass fasteners and a piece of yarn for a fastener. Staple the 2 strips of colored material to the back of the bag top. Staple end of material strips to the bottom of the bag.(4)

Use this grocery bag backpack to hold students' work sheets or projects. They may want to add banners or flags or foreign shields to their backpacks to make them more personal. Don't forget their names on the flap!

Use the patterns on the right to design shields, banners, or flags for the foreign country you are visiting.

cloth
straps

brass
fasteners

(4)

Keeping Track of My Travels

As you plan your foreign visit, fill in the two-week itinerary. **Place** would be where you are in that country. **Highlights** would be anything learned, special projects, etc. **Souvenirs** could also be projects or grades acquired on work. **Food** could be listed with approximate cost. **Total expenses** will help you become familiar with the currency of this country.

Date _____

Place _____

Highlights:

Souvenirs:

Food:

Total Expenses
_____

Date _____

Place _____

Highlights:

Souvenirs:

Food:

Total Expenses
_____

Date _____

Place _____

Highlights:

Souvenirs:

Food:

Total Expenses
_____

Date _____

Place _____

Highlights:

Souvenirs:

Food:

Total Expenses
_____

Date _____

Place _____

Highlights:

Souvenirs:

Food:

Total Expenses
_____

Date _____

Place _____

Highlights:

Souvenirs:

Food:

Total Expenses
_____

Date _____

Place _____

Highlights:

Souvenirs:

Food:

Total Expenses
_____

Date _____

Place _____

Highlights:

Souvenirs:

Food:

Total Expenses
_____

DESIGN YOUR OWN

Duplicate these patterns on heavy paper. Glue several thicknesses together or glue to cardboard to make them sturdy. Color these basic dolls. Cut slits in the feet for a circular cardboard stand. Add the ethnic costumes for each country you study.

Ethnic Costume

FOREIGN FACTS and DATA

Use this chart for planning. Then enlarge it to fit a bulletin board or large wall. Add the needed information. Students can then compare the data. Some of the data could be used to have students write a summary of what they have learned about their worldwide travel.

	Continent	Population	Capital City	Climate	Foods	Currency	Language	Religions	Festivals	Sports
Japan										
Italy										
Peru										
Kenya										
Norway										
India										
Quebec										

x

Tips for the Tour Guide

The name Norway comes from a Viking word meaning "way to the North." The Vikings followed the Norwegian shores to the north. The land is beautiful with sharp cliffs, waterfalls, glaciers, deep lakes and high flat lands abounding. Only a little of the land is flat enough to be farmed; therefore, the Norwegians use the sea for food. They call it their "blue meadow."

Some of the mountains in southern Norway are the highest mountains in Europe north of the Alps. Some of the tops of the mountains are not peaks but flat at the top.

Fjords and islands form the western shores. The North Atlantic Current flows over the sea and brings warm air even as far as Hammerfest in the north.

About half of Norway is north of the Arctic Circle. The width of the country can vary from 4 to 280 miles. The length of the country is 1100 miles long.

Shipping, fishing and shipbuilding keep up the economy. Now oil has been found off shore in the North Sea. This, also, will have a great influence on the economy.

The Vikings have given the Norwegians a hearty and courageous past. Their explorations have influenced the whole world.

The majority of Laplanders are considered Norwegian, although they seldom travel to south of the Arctic Circle. Their economy is based on herding and lumbering and has little effect on the total country of Norway.

Norwegians enjoy festivals and holidays. They are wonderful artisans. Many of the festivals and arts and crafts are influenced by the seasons and religion. The long, dark winters and short, sunlit summers give Norway the nickname of "Land of the Midnight Sun."

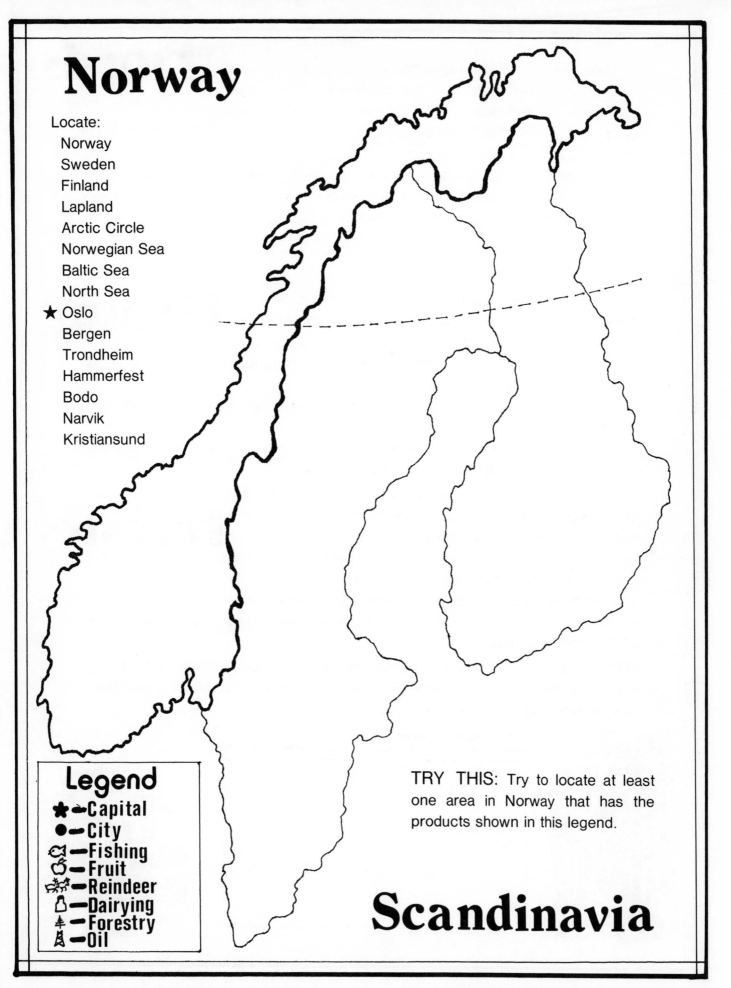

Norway

Locate:
- Norway
- Sweden
- Finland
- Lapland
- Arctic Circle
- Norwegian Sea
- Baltic Sea
- North Sea
- ★ Oslo
- Bergen
- Trondheim
- Hammerfest
- Bodo
- Narvik
- Kristiansund

Legend
- ★—Capital
- ●—City
- —Fishing
- —Fruit
- —Reindeer
- —Dairying
- —Forestry
- —Oil

TRY THIS: Try to locate at least one area in Norway that has the products shown in this legend.

Scandinavia

Fjords

Along Norways western coastline are the famous **fjords**. These are deep inlets into the mountains. There are thousands of islands along the shoreline, also. Both the fjords and islands help break up the waves and storms that blow over the North Atlantic Ocean.

The capital city of Oslo was built on a fjord, later named the Oslo Fjord.

Fjords can be only a few hundred yards wide with steep cliffs on each side or very wide for large ocean-going ships to enter.

Fishing

The famous fjords, warm waters of the North Atlantic Ocean and islands offshore all add to the reasons that Norway's fishing industry is the best in the world. Large factory ships spend weeks at sea and process the fish right on board the ship. Some fish is canned, some salted, and some frozen for sale.

Sport salmon fishing is popular in Norway and brings many fishermen from Europe.

Whaling has been done in Norway for hundreds of years. Because of the scarcity of whales, the Norwegians no longer harvest them.

Forestry

Pulp and paper industries are important to Norway. Most of the trees are spruce and pine. It is easy to transport the logs out of the mountainsides because of the many lakes and rivers. The logs can be easily floated down the mountainsides. The water also produces hydroelectric power for the mills.

Newspaper, magazine paper and packaging paper are the main products.

The Norwegians are very sensitive to their environments and always replant trees as they are harvested.

TRY THIS: Make a diorama in a small box showing fishing, forestry or the fjords of Norway. Try to make the scene as authentic and three-dimensional as possible. Use the box below to make a sketch of your diorama.

diorama sketch

There are four main festivals in Norway. **Syttende Mai** (Seventeenth of May) remembers the signing of the Norwegian Constitution. Parades, flags and bands lead the children through the steets of every city and town. Many activities are also planned such as dances, sports and dining.

June 24 is the **Midsummer Festival**. This feast is in honor of the sun. Bonfires are lighted to scare off evil creatures; birch boughs decorate the houses to represent new life in springtime. People go to enjoy fireworks displays, singing and dancing. Booths serve sausages, coffee and drinks. Everyone stays up to see the sunrise on the shortest night of the year!

St. Olaf Day on July 29 remembers the day St. Olav died. He was the King of Norway and died in battle in the year 1030. He became a symbol of everything good in Norway. People claim miracles have occurred at his grave site. On July 29 there is much celebrating with fireworks and games.

The most popular holiday is **Christmas**. On Christmas Eve, the tree is decorated with tinsel, lights, yarn dolls and miniature Norwegian flags. A special dinner of lutefisk, lefse or pork is served. Ice cream or rice pudding may also be served. A lucky almond is placed in the pudding. Someone may dress like **Julenissen** (Father Christmas) and deliver presents to the children. Most families go to a Lutheran church service either on Christmas Eve or Christmas Day. Celebrations and parties are held all through the Christmas season.

TRY THIS: Make a banner of Norwegian flags to string across your classroom or border a bulletin board.

Try making a yarn doll. Need: 10 red yarn pieces (18"—body); 10 red yarn pieces (6"—arms); 6 red yarn pieces (4"—for tying); 2 triangles of red felt (hat); small ball polyester stuffing (hat and beard); 2 movable eyes; 1 small circle pink felt (face). Fold over 10 long pieces of yarn. Tie at fold to form head. Slip 10 medium yarn pieces into loop for arms. Tie with short yarn. Tie ends of legs for feet. Add pink felt for face. Glue on eyes and beard. Glue pointed triangular hat with polyester fringe to the head. Attach a red yarn loop and hang on a bulletin board or between banners on a wire.

A.

B.

C.

D.

Viking Voyage

About 900 years ago the Viking sailing fleets sailed from the fjords to explore the seas around them. The Vikings were explorers, warriors and merchants who influenced the world that they knew. Some of the early Vikings were feared. One reason was because they were excellent sailors. Their boats were shallow and could go far inland on the rivers. They raided all along the shores of Western Europe, the Black Sea and Russia. While they were sailing, their travels took them to Iceland, Greenland and North America. Their culture was carried everywhere they went.

Other. Vikings were farmers and traders and not the wild men of the sea. There were not many roads over the mountains, so the people were forced to go by boat. The Norsemen were expert boatbuilders.

The amazing Viking ships were never more than 77 feet long (23.5 meters). The Vikings traveled far, without compasses, in ships powered only by oars and one sail. During battles, shields were hung over the sides of the ships. The figurehead at the front of the ship was usually a dragon.

TRY THIS: Make a Viking ship. Cut this pattern out of construction paper. Laminate it or apply clear self-adhesive paper. Glue or tape together. Staple 2 strips of stiff cardboard into the bottom to hold the mast. Use 1 chopstick for the mast. Attach a paper sail that has been decorated. Curve the paper when attaching so the air can catch the sail. Try sailing your ship in a tub, sink or pool of water. Add shields to the sides if you decide to have the Battle of the Boats!

CUT TWO MAST HOLDERS. GLUE TABS TO SIDES OF BOAT.

CUT TWO SIDES.

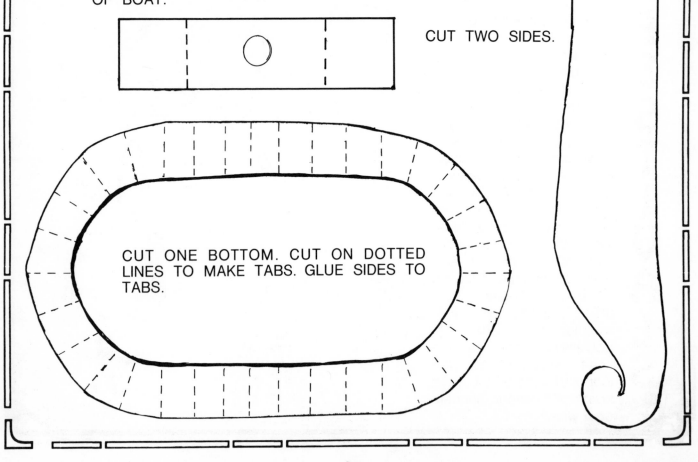

CUT ONE BOTTOM. CUT ON DOTTED LINES TO MAKE TABS. GLUE SIDES TO TABS.

Nibbling Norwegian Nourishment

Nibbling is a favorite pastime of Norwegians. They enjoy such delicacies as herring, goat cheese and **lutefisk** (lye fish). Lutefisk is a mixture of dried cod and salt that is served with melted butter and potatoes.

Goat cheese and the smelly **gammelost** (old cheese) are also favorites. Gammelost is a greenish-brown color.

Other favorite Norwegian dishes are **rommegrot**, which is a pudding made of boiled and thickened fresh cream and flour. Cinnamon and sugar are sprinkled on top. This is a favorite of the children. **Farikal**, mutton and cabbage; **fiskekaker**, codfish cakes; **lefse**, potato pancakes; and **gravlaks**, smoked salmon, are all favorites.

Adults like a strong drink called **akevitt** made from caraway seeds and potatoes. When a toast is given at a party, the word **skoal** is used to mean "to your health!"

TRY THIS: Christmastime also brings many special foods and at least seven different kinds of cookies. Rosettes are one kind of cookie that Norwegians make. Try the recipe below. You will need an adult to help you.

	Need:	Rosette iron	
		Cooking oil	
		2 eggs, slightly beaten	1 cup flour
		2 tsp. sugar	1 tbsp. lemon extract
		¼ tsp. salt	confectioners' sugar
		1 cup milk	

Add sugar to slightly beaten eggs; then add milk. Sift flour with salt. Stir into first mixture and beat until smooth. Add flavoring.

Dip heated iron into hot fat. (Fat should be hot enough to brown a piece of bread in 1 minute.) Dip iron in batter. Plunge batter-coated iron quickly into hot fat and cook from 2-3 minutes (until bubbling stops). Remove from iron and drain on brown paper. While still warm, dip in confectioners' sugar.

LAPLAND···

Lapland is not a nation. It is an area north of the Arctic Circle near the North Pole. Lapland is made up of the northern parts of Norway, Sweden, Finland and Russia. There are only about 35,000 people in this large area and most of them live in Norway.

Winter lasts nine months of the year and then spring comes for the other three months. During the winter there are two months when it is entirely dark. In two months of the spring, the sun never sets and it is light all of the time. This is known as the "midnight sun."

Most of the families raise reindeer. The deer are partly wild and partly tame. The reindeer herders move with the deer looking for new food. Because some have no permanent home, they are known as nomads. Nowadays most herders have a small home in a little village. Reindeer and wooden sleds are used for transportation when looking for the reindeer herds.

Laplanders that are not reindeer herders may be fishermen or work in the lumber mills. There are also iron mines near Kiruna and Gallivare. Find these cities on your map. Place the legend symbol for iron near the city names.

LAND OF THE MIDNIGHT SUN

Clothing must be warm in this cold climate. Most clothing is made of reindeer skins and wool. The clothing is very colorful in bright blue, red and yellow. The hat worn by the men and boys is called the "hat of the four winds." It has four corners that hang down in the back. Grass is placed inside the reindeer skin moccasins as insulation from the cold. It also absorbs moisture and is soft to walk on.

1   2   3   4   5   6

TRY THIS: Make a "hat of the four winds." 1. Use one full sheet of newspaper to make the hat band. 2. Fold it in half lengthwise twice. 3. Staple to the correct head size to fit over the ears. Cut one full sheet of newspaper in half. Fold into 2 double triangular shapes. 4. Staple the triangular point into the inside of the hatband. 5. Place 1 triangle in the front of the band and one in the back. 6. The front triangle will fold over the top of the band and the back triangle will fold over the back of the band. Staple the four corners together in the back of the hat to form a tail.

Decorate the hat with brightly colored construction paper or tempera paint. Discuss pattern and repetition before you begin.

TRY THIS: Make a pair of **skallers** (moccasins) by enlarging this pattern. Make them double from brown wrapping paper, staple together and decorate with yarn or paint. Stuff them with dry grass and use as a border on a bulletin board. Can you guess why the toe curls up at the end? _____

_____

A lemming is a tiny animal with yellow and black or gray fur. It is a member of the rodent family. Lemmings seldom come out of their nests except at night. A female can have as many as twenty-five babies a year. That is quite a family for the nest!

Lemmings migrate when they get too crowded—about every three to four years. They eat almost anything along the way. For some reason, unknown to man, the lemmings migrate toward the sea. When they get to the edge of the seaside cliffs, they are pushed over by the other lemmings following them. The few lemmings left at the end are the lucky ones. They build nests, have more little lemmings and start over again.

Other wild animals native to Norway are the wolf, lynx, otter, fox and even bear. Seabirds are plentiful. Puffins and ptarmigans are often seen. Puffins are interesting and incredible birds. They nest in rabbit holes after they have first chased away the rabbits. They have very strong, hooked yellow beaks, black and white feathers and red feet. When the female has young, the beak becomes enlarged and she may carry up to six fish crosswise. She returns home to feed her young. If a female is killed, another puffin will take over the care of the young. When they are old enough to fish for themselves, the female's beak shrinks back to normal size.

TRY THIS: Make a maze for the lemmings to find their way to the sea. Remember there can only be one way to get there! When you are finished, have a friend try out your maze.

THE SEA

START

LEMMINGS

Skiing

Skiing is the most popular sport in Norway. Norwegians can always get around in winter since skiing is also a practical way of traveling.

In the days of Norsemen, skiing was considered a sport of kings. This is not true today as almost everyone in Norway is an enthusiastic skier. Today huge crowds gather outside of Oslo at the ski-jumping hill. The skiers race down the hill and fly off the end of the jump into mid air.

The Norwegian army held skiing competitions as long ago as 1843. The love of the sport grew so rapidly that at least 4000 skiers took part in the events in 1880. Skiing was exported to other countries by the Norwegians who immigrated abroad. Now skiing is popular all over the world.

Ice skating is also popular in Norway. The Norwegian Olympic medalist Sonja Henie brought the beauty of figure skating to the world. Find out more about her.

TRY THIS: The Winter Olympic Games include many skiing events. Find out the names of the events and the number of times Norway has won a gold medal in each event. Use the chart below. In the circle, draw the Olympic logo for skiing. Perhaps you would like to compare the U.S.A. and Norwegian medalists.

Norwegian Olympic Medals

TROLLS &

Many of Norway's stories about gnomes and trolls come from the forests along the Oslo Fjord. The whispering of the wind in the evergreen trees helps your imagination.

Long ago gnomes were seen regularly by all kinds of people. Now they have been forced to live below the ground and keep out of sight for fear they will be killed. You may not be able to see them, but they are there!

The first statue of a gnome was discovered in Norway. The inscription read "Nisse." The statue had been carved from a tree root.

Gnomes, when accidently seen, look like a miniature person wearing a red cap and blue shirt. They have white beards and wear green pants.

Gnomes work in the woods at night and sometimes in homes and barns. If the barn gnomes are treated well, they keep an eye on livestock and crops. Gnomes have special friendships with animals. They can help the sick animals feel better and protect the animals from their enemies. They claim to be seven times stronger than a man and can smell nineteen times better with their noses.

Trolls are ugly, large creatures. They usually have one eye and a carrot-shaped nose. Their hair is black and looks as if it had never been washed or brushed. The trolls usually cause trouble wherever they go. They tease and torment the gnomes and humans. They can definitely make a Monday a "bad day!"

TRY THIS: Gnomes like to play Tug of War, perhaps because they are so strong. Choose two teams of gnomes and two teams of trolls. Have a Tug of War to see which team is the strongest.

GNOMES

Gremlins are relatively modern "little people." In the circles below, try to find and sketch a picture of these "little people": gremlins, gnomes, trolls, dwarfs, elves, and leprechauns.

TRY THIS: Make simple costumes and masks and act out how a gnome would act helping a sick animal; how a troll would act at a human's dinner table, etc.

After studying more about these "little people," set up teams to debate the question, "Are gnomes and trolls real?"

ROSEMALING

Norway has many talented artists and craftsmen. The long winters seem to be the times when the Norwegians can practice their crafts.

One of the best known crafts is **rosemaling**. This is the art of rose painting. In the 1700's, the artists, always men, traveled from home to home painting walls, ceilings, chests, etc. They never signed their paintings as other artists did, but each had his own style of painting. These different styles of rosemaling depended on the part of Norway the painter was from. Farmers used to paint their walls and furniture with flowers. Now rosemalers paint on all kinds of things.

The colors used in rosemaling are usually tones of blue, red, gold, dark green and accented with black or white.

TRY THIS: Transfer the pattern below onto a nine-inch paper plate and paint as a rosemaler would do. Be patient and you will be pleased with your work!

NORWAY

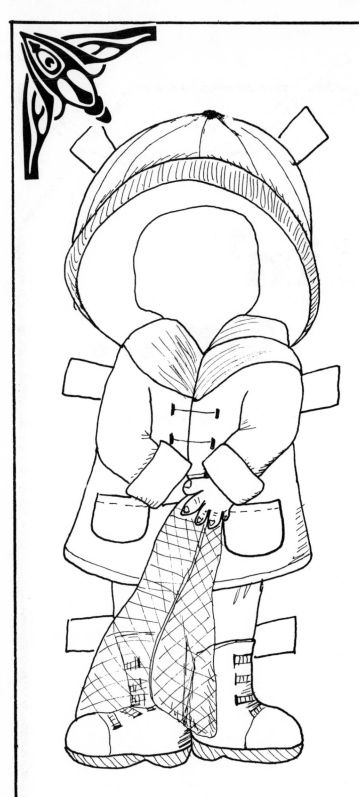

Color the costume on the left. Design your own Norwegian costume on the right. Color carefully. Try the completed costume on the doll.

Travelin' On ...

The following is a list of additional topics that interested or highly motivated students may want to learn more about:

Oil
Postage stamps
Ptarmigan birds
Norwegian language
Black Death
World War II
Royalty of Norway
Borgund church
Education
Camps for Children
Cheesemaking
Lichens
"Birch Legs"
Medical care
Norwegian Nobel prize winners
UNICEF
Peer Gynt
Edvard Grieg
Edvard Munch

Japan

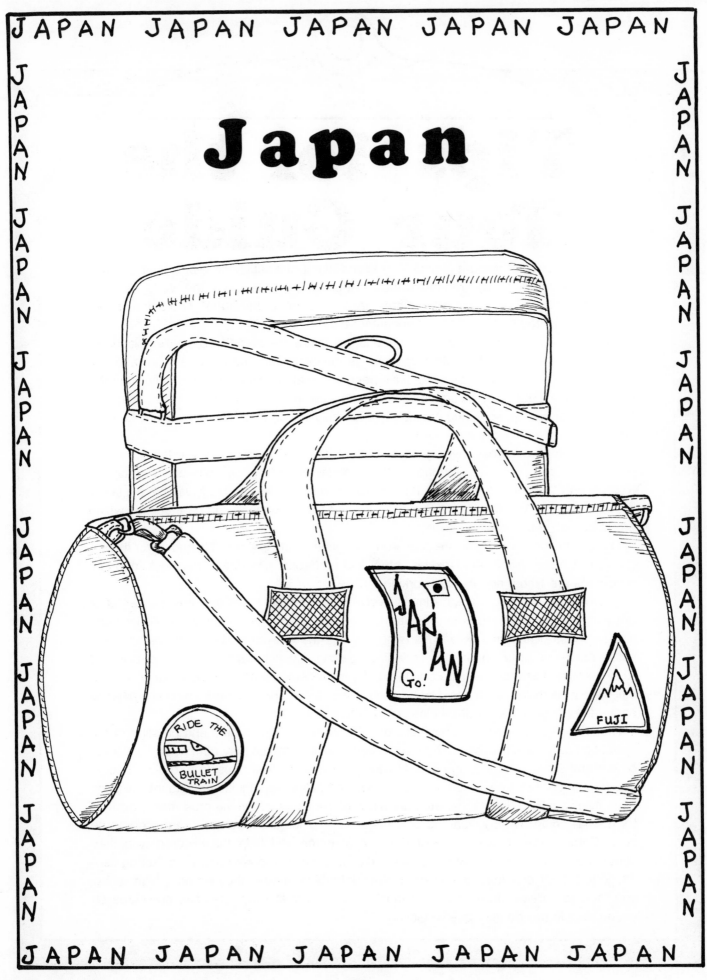

Tips for the Tour Guide

In a relatively short amount of time after World War II, the Japanese rebuilt their land and also their economy. They are among the most progressive people in the world, yet they treasure tradition. They travel in the fastest train in the world, the **Bullet**, and see rice paddies being planted by hand as their ancestors did.

The four main islands of Japan are quite large. There are over 3000 smaller islands as well—some are uninhabited. Most of Japan is mountainous. The most famous mountain peak is Mt. Fuji. Over fifty volcanoes have been active at one time, although only nine have erupted since 1958. The natural hot springs are a favorite vacation spot for the Japanese.

Most Japanese are seafaring people because they live so close to the sea. Shipbuilders and fishermen are important to the economy.

Honshu has the largest lowland areas and has the best farmland. Three-fourths of the people live on it. Terracing is done on the mountainsides to grow fruits and vegetables. Kyushu and Shikoku are farther south and have a warmer climate. They also have a faster growing season. Weather can also be severe and bring typhoons and earthquakes which are followed by tidal waves.

The chief minerals in Japan are coal, iron, manganese and copper. It is known for its production of heavy machinery, textiles, steel and electronic products. The most important resources are timber and its hardworking people.

Tokyo is the capital of Japan. Almost twelve million people live there. It is the center of government, but also the center of culture. The Ginza is a famous shopping, entertainment and business district in Tokyo. This large city has the environmental problems other big cities have—air pollution, noise, crowding, garbage, water supply, etc. The cities of Kitakyushu and Shimonoseki are connected by an undersea tunnel. Transportation in most cities is done mainly on trains. During rush times, there are "pushers" who are hired to shove the passengers into the trains so no space is wasted.

The jobs Japanese workers have are directly related to the amount and prestige of the education they have received. The most prestigious companies may not pay high salaries, by our standards, but the fringe benefits are great. Usually free housing or reduced housing, free lunch, free transportation to and from work, clothing, athletic equipment, wedding gifts, free vacations, insurance, etc., are a few of the benefits. On the other hand, working for a small company may mean no benefits at all. Women are moving into the work force now. Before, women were expected to be at home and help the children with their schoolwork. If the children did not do well on exams, the women were blamed. Young people go to school for at least nine years. Exams determine whether they will go to high school and then to college. Japan has an almost 100 percent literacy rate. The pressures on young people can be very overwhelming.

Identify the following on the map:

Hokkaido   Honshu
Shikoku   Kyushu

Using the symbols provided, locate the following:

✳ **Capital**

Tokyo

○ **Cities**

Nagasaki   Hiroshima
Kyoto   Yokohama
Sapporo   Sendai
Osaka   Kushiro

▲▲ **Mountains**

Mt. Fuji

〰 **Waters**

Sea of Japan   Korea Strait
Pacific Ocean East China Sea

Japan has a long coastline with many inlets. If a string was laid along the coast and then stretched, it would reach almost three-fourths of the way around the world.

JAPAN

Color the circle red in this flag. Leave the field white. Japan is known as the "land of the sun." By looking at the flag, can you tell why it is a good respresentation of Japan?

_____

_____

19

JAPANESE

Rice is eaten at every meal, just as bread is eaten in the United States. There is a great variety of vegetables and fish eaten also in the Japanese home. They have never eaten much meat because there is not much land to raise beef cattle and also Buddhism forbids the killing of animals. Soybeans are often eaten in place of meat.

The Japanese menu for a Japanese family might be:

      Breakfast—bean soup, rice, egg, pickles, tea.

      Lunch—noodles, pickled vegetables, soy sauce, tea.

      Supper—stew of meat or seafood, bean curd, vegetables, rice.

The Japanese do not eat desserts (**kyogashi**) at mealtime. They are usually eaten only on special occasions such as birthdays or weddings.

A game with chopsticks and dried beans can be lots of fun. Each player tries to pick up as many beans as he can in two minutes. You can crown the national Chopstick Champion with a crown held together with chopsticks!

COOKING

22

The traditional clothing for special occasions is the kimono. It is a one-piece, loose-fitting robe with wide sleeves. A sash, or **obi**, is used as a belt. Boys may wear short kimono shirts called **hakama**. On their feet are **geta**, or wooden clogs. They may also wear sandals called **zor**. Design your own kimonos below.

JAPAN

Sports and

The workweek has been shortened for the Japanese and people are thinking more now about what to do with their leisure time. In Japan a person's hobby may be a traditional Japanese one or a modern one borrowed from the United States.

Baseball has become Japan's national game. The Japanese enjoy many sports including soccer, football, basketball, volleyball, tennis, hockey, swimming and skiing. Golf is a current fad and expensive sport in Japan. Bowling is much less expensive and is becoming more popular.

The Japanese version of the pinball game is called **pachinko**. There are a million of these machines in Japan. This is a form of gambling done from early morning to late at night.

Circle the sports words as you find them in this word search.

Team Sports

BASEBALL
MOVIES
GOLF
BOWLING
TRACK
PACHINKO
SKIING
MOUNTAIN
  CLIMBING

SWIMMING
TENNIS
VOLLEYBALL
FOOTBALL
BASKETBALL
SOCCER
HOCKEY

```
B C A E F H I O Z S T M E A S T R
O M S R G B L I P A C H I N K O T
T E R O M N Y L A F G O E A I F S
G H T I V L F M N S W I M M I N G
S R I R V O L L E Y B A L L N O R
L E H B A S E B A L L C K E G Y O
W Y S O C C E R Y F O O T B A L L
C E L W I M K B L I N G T I S S O
T K E L N N M O V I E S I N N E T
V C O I L L G E Y G N I S S I N T
M O U N T A I N C L I M B I N G A
E H I G O N U Y L T S R D E O F V
F I H S B A S K E T B A L L F V I
N P U V E R S T A N R S V U N D N
R V I U Y O L M S E R L I E M O D
```

24

Self-Defense

Sumo Wrestling

Thousands of people watch the championship sumo wrestling matches. The wrestlers are very large men, fed a special diet. Sumo follows a lengthy, formal ceremony. It is very fast and the action is over in seconds. The match is decided when one wrestler is pushed, dropped or brought to the ground. The only part of the body that can touch the ground is the sole of the foot. A sumo wrestling match is a combination of physical power, showmanship and skill.

Kendo

Kendo is bamboo sword fighting using the methods of the **samurai** or warriors. Kendo is taught in schools to the very young. The contestant wears armor and scores points by hitting his opponent's body.

Judo and Karate

Judo means "the gentle way." Karate means "empty hands." Karate is a style of fighting using jabs, hits and kicks with the elbows, hands and feet. It is so dangerous that when young children are learning the sport, they practice on wood rather than each other.

Judo specialists move through stages of learning that are noted by the color of the belt of their uniforms. The colors progress from white, yellow, orange, green, blue, brown and then to the black belt—or highest honor.

On the back of this sheet, write a short, imaginative story about how Chinko the Carp became a sumo wrestler or a black belt in judo. Illustrate Chinko in his uniform.

Fishing

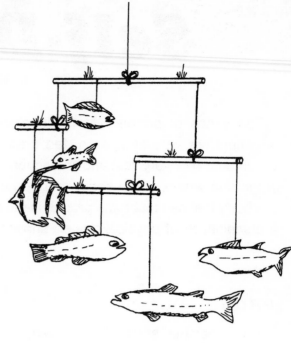

Japan is one of the world's greatest fishing countries. The fishermen catch about 2500 tons of fish each day. They catch from tiny sardines to huge tuna—well over sixty-three different varieties of fish.

The Japanese eat twice as much fish as any other country in the world. An unusual form of night fishing goes on in Gifu. Crowds of people gather in the light of flaming torches to watch the trained cormorants do the fishing.

Oysters are also harvested by women called **ama**. They may dive to the depths of 45 feet with no oxygen equipment. Oyster farming also produces more than 200 million pearls each year.

Make a fish mobile: Research at least six unusual fish living in the waters from the Aleutian Islands to Africa. Draw these fish as accurately as you can, including many details. Outline the fish and details with a black magic marker. Glue small, torn pieces of tissue paper to the fish—trying to keep the true colors. On the back write several sentences about this particular variety of fish. Then paint gesso or a solution of white glue and water over the entire fish. This will make the fish look shiny. Attach and balance the fish using plastic straws and thread.

Turn a table into an underwater scene. Research which fish would be near the surface, in the middle, and on the bottom of the ocean. Each constructs a fish, using much color. Attach with string under the table. Use a piece of natural burlap or the floor for the ocean bottom. Add shells, weeds, etc. You may want to have an **ama** diving for oysters, too. Cover the sides of the table with paper or burlap. Cut circles in the side to use as portholes. Attach cardboard circles for support for the portholes. Add cellophane of different colors to look through if you like. Then take a peek!

Inside   Outside

CHANOYU

Japanese Tea

The tea ceremony is known for its silence, meditation and rest, and respect. Japanese women study for years to learn the many steps of the ceremony. Few women achieve the "master of tea" degree.

These are simplified steps to the complicated ceremony. Perhaps you could practice this simple ceremony with a friend.

First, serve a small sweet piece of candy while you arrange the utensils.

Now, clean the ladle with a red cloth napkin.

Third, wipe the rim of the bowl with a white cloth.

Fourth, warm the bowl with hot water. Dip out the water with a ladle.

Now, scoop powdered tea from a small box into the bowl.

Next, ladle the boiling water into the bowl and stir the tea until it foams.

Then turn the bowl one and one-half times around and serve the first guest.

This first guest asks the others, "May I drink first?" The rest reply, "Yes."

Last, the first guest bows, takes three sips and inhales deeply. On the last sip, it is polite to make a slurping noise to please the hostess.

Below draw a picture of the equipment needed for the tea ceremony. Be sure to decorate the teapot and cups. Remember, there are no handles on the cups.

Ceremony

The poetry form of haiku was developed in Japan and later became popular in the United States. It tells a story or makes a picture in your mind of something that happens in nature. Many descriptive words are used in this seventeen-syllable poem. Usually haiku is written in three lines.

Line 1: tells where the poem takes place (5 syllables)
Line 2: tells what is going on (7 syllables)
Line 3: an ending or feeling is written (5 syllables)

Try to write a haiku poem. Some things in nature you may want to write about are butterflies, flowers, trees, birds, carp, goldfish, Mt. Fuji, the sun, caterpillars, fall, string, etc. Trace the shape of the fan on this paper. Write your poetry on it. Draw and paint a picture to go with your poetry. Glue this paper onto heavy cardboard or a piece of styrofoam (meat tray). Attach a handle and make a flat fan.

Tanka is also a form of Japanese poetry. It is a five-line poem using a 5-syllable, 7-syllable, 5-syllable, 7-syllable, and 7-syllable pattern. This is a total of thirty-one syllables.

Japan at War

The Japanese had military power and were successful in wars against China, Russia and Germany. Military men were honored. During World War II the Japanese became allies of the German and Italian people. They were successful in their efforts during the war. They made a surprise attack on America when they bombed Pearl Harbor in Hawaii. Air raids on Japanese cities began. After four years of terrible war and the atomic bombing of two Japanese cities, the Japanese surrendered. Japan was ruined. The bombed cities were in rubble. Scientists predicted nothing would grow there for seventy years. However, within three years the trees were getting leaves.

Today the Japanese constitution outlaws war. Only 5 percent of the government's money is spent on defense. The money that they have has been used to help the country grow and develop technically. Japan is the third largest economic country in the world.

The feelings of the Japanese people about war are understandable when we realize they are the only people ever bombed by nuclear weapons. They never want to see that terrible suffering and destruction happen again.

You may need to do more reading or researching of information about the Japanese in the World War in order to do this activity.

Pretend you are writing a newspaper article about one of these topics: Pearl Harbor, air power, suicide pilots, Hiroshima, Nagasaki, or nuclear bombs.

A good reporter always includes who, what, when, where, and why information in the story. You may want to include a "photo" to make people interested in your story.

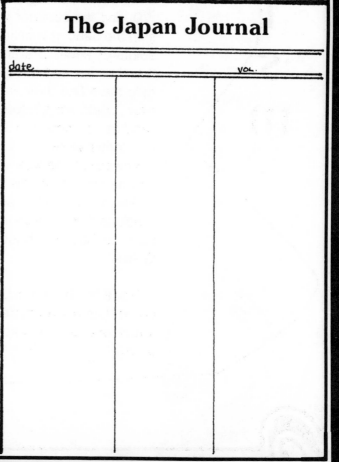

The Japan Journal

date   vol.

Buddhism

Buddhism has greatly influenced Japanese culture. It stresses self-discipline. It is opposed to killing and stresses the belief that everything is linked to one another. There are approximately 82 million Buddhists in Japan.

A Buddhist funeral includes cremation, and a funeral ceremony continues for several days. Relatives and friends keep a vigil beside the dead person all night before the funeral.

During the summer a festival is held to worship the dead. It is called the Bon Festival. The spirits of ancestors are believed to return to their homes, and paper lanterns are lighted to help them find their way. When the festival is over, boats are floated to the sea with lighted candles to show the spirits the way back to the "other world."

Nowadays, people visit their former homes and neighbors on this day.

Try to find out something about other religions that are also important in Japan today such as Shinto, Christianity, Tenrikyo, Sokka Gakkai.

Trace the large Buddah shape for a booklet cover. Cut writing paper to fit the shape. Write about one of the Japanese religions in the booklet.

HIRAGANA

The Japanese borrowed early Chinese picture writing. They used the Chinese characters, called **kanji**, to represent ideas in their own spoken language. By the sixth grade, a student should know 900 kanji.

The Japanese also learn two other written languages, **hiragana** and **katakana**. Each of these languages has forty-eight characters. Also, most seventh grade students begin to learn English.

A few people have suggested that this complicated language be reduced to an alphabet such as is used in English. But most Japanese would not change. They feel they would lose their heritage.

The Japanese have invented a typewriter for their writing, but it is so large that it cannot be used easily. Handwritten letters, done in calligraphy, are widely accepted.

Below are some Japanese words and phrases written in "Romanization" or Latin letters. Make a greeting card to send to a friend or relative. Use as many Japanese words as you can. Add pictures and color to make your card attractive.

Hello	Konnichiwa
Please	Dozo
I love you	Watashi wa anata
How are you?	Ikaga desuka?
Thank you	Arigato
Good-bye	Sayonara
mother	haha
father	chichi
brother	kyodai
sister	shimai
teacher	kyoshi
friend	tomodachi

KANJI

JAPAN

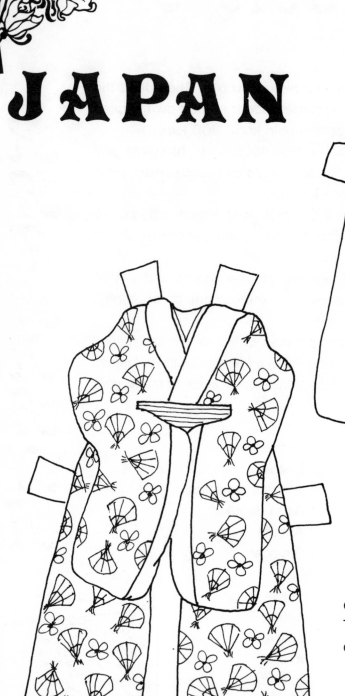

Color the costume on the left.
Design your own Japanese costume on the right. Color carefully. Try the completed costume on the doll.

Travelin' On ...

The following is a list of additional topics that interested or highly motivated students may want to learn more about:

Origami
Cherry blossoms
Calligraphy
Karate
World War II aircraft
Japanese current
Fishing
Whaling
Cormorant birds
Pearl divers
Foods
Obi, etc.
Flower arranging
Baseball
Transportation
Mt. Fuji
Tidal waves
Yen
Feudal system
Ginza
Environmental problems
Economic concerns
Educational system
Careers
Cultured pearls
Working women
Silk
Bath ritual
Arranged marriages
National holidays
Kabuki
Bunraku
No
Japanese gardening
Shintoism

Kenya

Tips for the Tour Guide

Kenya was named after its famous mountain, Mount Kenya. Kenya is located in East Africa and the equator divides the continent in half. There are four main geographical areas: the Coast, along the Indian Ocean with a coral reef; the Bush, with low thorn trees and scrub brush that covers most of Kenya; the Highlands, high plateaus, more rainfall and better soil; Great Rift Valley, along the entire length of Kenya.

Nairobi is Kenya's capital city. It is the site of many tourist safaris. The largest groups of people in Kenya are the Kikuyu, the Luo, the Luhya and the Masai. There are also many Europeans, Asians and Arabs residing in Kenya.

Swahili is the national language. Many other common African languages are used. The majority of Kenyans are animists, but other religious beliefs are also represented.

Education has made a slow move forward. The number of schools has increased and now education is free for all Kenyans.

Most Kenyans are farmers. Kenya exports coffee, tea, sisal and pyrethrum. The major industry is tourism. The pleasant climate and wild game parks are the major attractions.

Tsavo National Game Park is the largest preserve. One of the most interesting parks is Nairobi National Park located a few miles from the capital.

The Arabs, Portuguese, and British influenced the growth and development of Kenya. On December 12, 1963, Kenya became an independent republic under the leadership of Jomo Kenyatta.

There are approximately 18,000,000 people living in Kenya today. The Kenya shilling is the unit of currency. National holidays that are observed are the following: December 12—Uhura Day (Independence Day), October 20—Kenyatta Day.

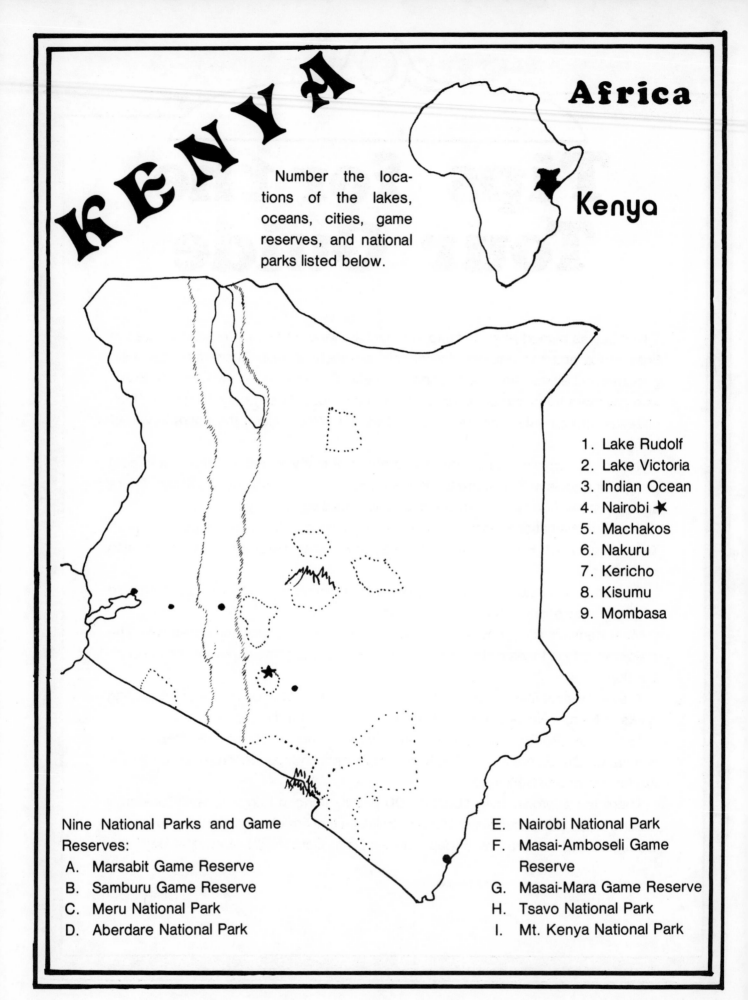

KENYA

Africa

Kenya

Number the locations of the lakes, oceans, cities, game reserves, and national parks listed below.

1. Lake Rudolf
2. Lake Victoria
3. Indian Ocean
4. Nairobi ✱
5. Machakos
6. Nakuru
7. Kericho
8. Kisumu
9. Mombasa

Nine National Parks and Game Reserves:
A. Marsabit Game Reserve
B. Samburu Game Reserve
C. Meru National Park
D. Aberdare National Park

E. Nairobi National Park
F. Masai-Amboseli Game Reserve
G. Masai-Mara Game Reserve
H. Tsavo National Park
I. Mt. Kenya National Park

"SHOOTING"

Kenya has eight national parks which contain the largest number of wild animals in the world. Many tourists visit Kenya each year just to see these herds of wild animals. Tourism is the second largest money-maker Kenya has. The **Nairobi National Park** is the smallest park and is located about five miles from the capital city. This park is unusual in that it has an Animal Orphanage. The orphanage takes care of animals that were separated from their mothers or abandoned. Not only does the orphanage save lives, but also provides a teaching area for Kenya's children, a research station and study area for university students. If these animals cannot make the change back to the wild, they are sold to zoos all over the world. **Tsavo National Park** is large and covers over 8000 square miles of wild country. The biggest wild game lives there—lions, buffalo and rhinoceroses. Elephants, giraffes and zebras are also there.

TRY THIS: No longer are tourists allowed to go on safaris to shoot the wild game. The only shooting done is with a camera. Pretend you are on a "shooting" safari. Show us the pictures you took. Are there several animals in your picture? What is the background like? Is there water nearby?

Papier maché a large-sized class animal. Display in your school lobby.

37

Hippopotomus

Kenya has many "creatures great and small." There is much to learn about each one. The National Geographic set called **Book of Mammals** is a good resource to find out more about these animals.

Hippos spend much of their time in water. Because they are such large animals (5000-8000 lbs.), their body weight is easier to move about in the water. Their eyes, ears and nostrils are located on top of their heads so that most of their bodies can be underwater, yet they can see, hear and breathe. The skin of the hippo gives off a red liquid, once thought to be blood. Baby hippos (calves) are born underwater and drink milk from their mothers underwater, also. They will climb on the mothers' backs to rest.

TRY THIS: Make a paper plate hippo with these instructions:

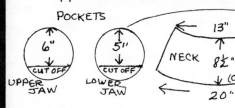

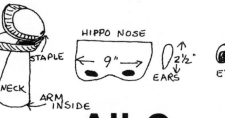

All Creatures

Each zebra has its own pattern of stripes just as fingerprints are different on humans. There are several ideas why zebras have stripes. Some scientists think that biting insects have a difficult time finding the zebras. There are three kinds of zebras whose stripes differ a lot. They are the mountain zebra, Grevy's zebra and plains zebra. The name "zebra" means tiger horse. They do have many of the same characteristics of horses. Young zebras' stripes are usually brown and white. They can run and play an hour after they are born.

TRY THIS: Plan carefully and design a poster advertising the World Wildlife Fund. Your class could collect money to be sent for the survival of wildlife in Africa. The address is:
WORLD WILDLIFE FUND
1601 Connecticut Ave., N.W.
Washington, D.C. 20009

Zebra

Lions of Africa live in groups called **prides**. They live together all of their lives except for male cubs who may take over other prides. Lions live in the grassy plains where herds of large animals roam. They hunt together to kill a large wildebeest or zebra. A lion's roar serves many purposes: it is a welcome to others in its pride, a call or command to come, or a warning to other prides to keep away. Newborn cubs have spotted, thick fur. Their eyes open after two or three days. They must stay hidden in the grasses until they are strong enough to keep up with the rest.

TRY THIS: The tribes use seeds to make necklaces. Use seeds and/or beans. String a necklace or belt after soaking the seeds in warm water. Make a self-hardening clay lion to string, also.

Lions

Great and Small

Wildebeests are also known as **gnus**. There are blue and black wildebeests. The colors are the only differences. Wildebeests are distinguished by their long neck hair and thick horns. They feed mainly on grasses. When the dry season arrives, the wildebeests must migrate, some-times more than 800 miles to find food. Wildebeests, especially new-born calves, seem to serve as a main food for faster, larger animals of the plains. Their main enemies are spotted hyenas, lions, cheetahs, leop-ards and wild dogs.

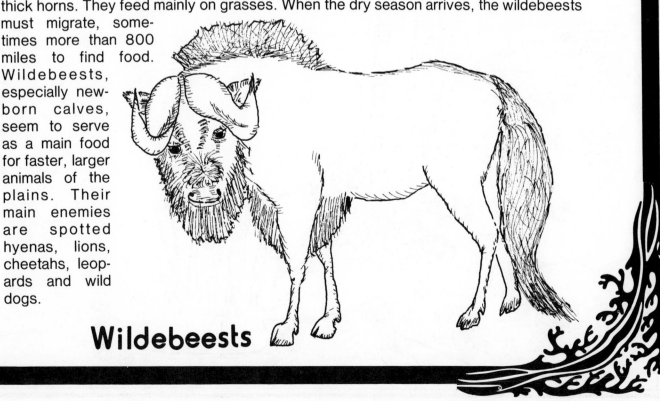

Wildebeests

CORAL REEF

The eastern shores of Kenya support the most abundant ocean life. Over 800 different species of tropical fish live in this warm water. The coral formations act as protection and food for these fish. Most fish in the reef are small, an inch or two long; fewer are more than a foot long. One larger kind of fish is the grouper. It waits silently and patiently for food to drift by. The smaller fish are very colorful. Red, green, orange, black-spotted, blue-and-white stripped in all shades and all different shapes are seen. These schools of fish are often very curious about skin divers and will often come very close and stare at them. Several species are the scorpion fish, moorish idol, pilot fish, zebra fish, red snapper, parrot fish, damsel fish, trumpet fish and sergeant majors. There are also sea anemones and starfish.

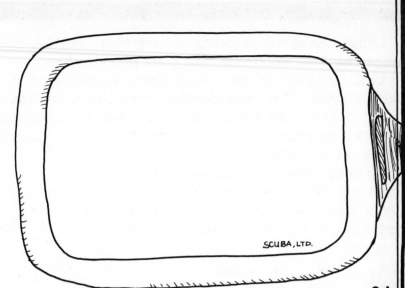

SCUBA, LTD.

National Park

TRY THIS: Draw what you think you would see through your snorkel mask while in the Coral Reef National Park. You may need to do a little research on the shapes of these fish so your picture can be as accurate as possible.

During certain seasons of the year, almost two million flamingos gather at Lake Nakuru. The male greater flamingo may be six feet tall and weigh almost sixty pounds. There are at least fifteen tons of algae being eaten every hour by these flamingos! The water in the lake is shallow and as the birds eat, they leave their droppings. These droppings can be as much as 60-80 tons each day! Quickly the warm, shallow water, filled with bacteria, produces the much-needed algae. This is a quick and efficient food cycle. The birds who eat the fish from this lake may eat up to 250,000 fish each day. The sight of all these flamingos feeding in the shallow lake is amazing. It seems as if there is not one spare inch of ground without a flamingo in it!

Flamingos build their nests on the open soda flats. The temperatures may reach over 100 degrees during the day. If the young do not die from the heat, they must be very cautious of their predators of marabou storks, tawny eagles and other large birds.

TRY THIS: Make a flamingo in its resting stance (one-legged). Need: 1 block of wood (approximately 2" x 5" x 1"), one piece of strong wire (8" long), thread, polyester stuffing, pink cloth, pink feathers, moveable eyes. Drill a small hole in the center of the wood block. Glue wire into hole. Sew the two pink cloth patterns together. Turn inside out. Stuff. Glue wire to inside of bird. Add details. Arrange all the flamingos on a large blue/green mirrored lake.

THE FLAMINGOS OF LAKE NAKURU

chopping

borer

Millions of years ago, Lake Victoria was larger. Gradually the ash from the active volcanoes began to fill in the lake. The ash, along with clay and sandstone, was an excellent fossil preserver. In 1931 Dr. Louis Leakey and his wife, Mary, found the fossil jawbone and skulls of several prehistoric individuals. This was a very important discovery because it showed that Africa had a Stone Age culture of prehistoric people. The Leakeys also found many fossil tools. Louis Leakey was not only an archaeologist interested in early remains, he also experimented with ways of making stone tools. Through this experimenting, he found how many early hunters and gatherers got their food.

TRY THIS: Make your own Stone Age tools, using stones, sticks and string, or strips of leather. Try doing different kinds of work with them. What worked best for you?

hand-axe

spear point

Dr. Leakey at Lake Victoria

Have your own archeological dig. Fill an area (sand box, plastic swimming pool, etc.) with sand. Hide "treasures" from your civilization in it. Examples would be a McDonald's cup or wrapper, old sneaker, earring, pizza cardboard circle, **TV Guide**, matchbox car, etc. Use small trowels, paintbrushes, spoons to dip up the area. Everything needs to be numbered and described in detail in a notebook as it is found.

The Baobab Tree

Although most of Kenya is very dry, there are no cacti. Instead there are plants called succulents. These plants have spiny limbs and store water. Water-storing plants are very important to all of Africa. The fig tree has large, long roots that soak up all the moisture in the area. Some taller plants collect rainwater in their leaves and then let it drip onto the ground slowly so more is absorbed. Most of Kenya is called the bush. It is a large area of low thorn trees, scrub brush and occasional baobab trees. Because of the lack of moisture and poor soil, the vegetation is sparse. The baobab tree is shaped like a bottle. The trunk is filled with moist pulp and can be as big as 30 ft. (9m.) in diameter. It is often eaten by animals during the dry season. It has no leaves during the dry season. Do you know why? During the rainy season, the baobab has large flowers, pollinated by bats, and oblong-shaped fruit. The fruit and leaves can be eaten. A legend about the unusual shape and lack of leaves on the baobab says that the Devil uprooted the tree and the branches are really the roots.

SUN-FLOWER   TOMATO   PUMPKIN   CARROT   BEANS   CORN

TRY THIS: Think of what a garden would look like if the plants were turned upside down. Include carrots, pumpkins, corn, beans, tomatoes, and sunflowers in your picture. Add any other plants you think would be interesting.

"Uhuru na Umoja"

In 1963 Kenya became a Republic and part of the British Commonwealth of Nations. Jomo Kenyatta became the first Prime Minister. Kenyatta worked all of his life bringing freedom to Kenya. He was most successful in achieving freedom and also unifying the many African tribes, Europeans, and Asians in the country. Kenyatta stressed the word, **Uhuru**, which means freedom. He also added the word **na Umoja**, which means unity.

When Kenya became a Republic, many of the minority groups worried about what would happen to them. Many retired Europeans had spent all of their lives in Kenya and really did not want to leave. When President Kenyatta took over, he asked these people to stay in Kenya and take citizenship there. About 60 percent of the people did choose to remain in Kenya.

The new flag of the Republic of Kenya is shown. Follow the description carefully as you color it.

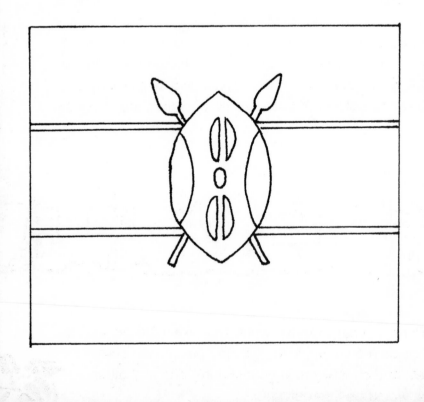

The field is made up of three horizontal stripes of black, red and green (top to bottom). Narrow white stripes separate the larger stripes.

In the center is an African shield colored in red, white and black. Under the shield are two crossed native spears.

This flag was adopted in 1963 when Kenya became an independent nation.

Why does the flag have a shield and spears on it?

_____

_____

44

SWAHILI LANGUAGE

There are about 1700 languages spoken on the African continent. Swahili is the most common language in the eastern part of Africa. Most people know Swahili along with their own ethnic language. The name "Swahili" originally came from the Arabic word meaning coast.

TRY THIS: Write four story problems about animals and Zumani the great hunter. Write inside the animal shapes below. Combine the counting words to make larger numbers also.

Counting words:
1—nne (n' nay)
2—tatu (ta' tu)
3—mbili (m bee' lee)
4—moja (mo' jah)
5—tano (tah' no)

6—sita (see' tah)
7—saba (sah' bah)
8—nane (nah' nay)
9—tisa (tee' sah)
10—kumi (koo' mee)

CITIES OF KENYA

People often talk of Nairobi and comment that it has the finest climate in the world. It's altitude is 5500 feet which makes the temperature so comfortable. Most days are warm, yet the night temperatures drop to about 45 degrees F.—very comfortable for sleeping. There are so many sunny days in Nairobi that it has become known as the "Garden City in the Sun." Nairobi is a relatively new city since it was founded in 1900. The name "Nairobi" means cold stream. The location was chosen because it was the last level ground before the railroad entered the high mountain country. Today Nairobi is a tourist city. From there many safaris take place.

Nairobi

TRY THIS: On the back of this paper, draw a picture of you and your friends leaving on a safari. You'll need photographic equipment!

Mombasa

The largest city on the coast of the Indian Ocean is Mombasa. It is really located on an island and is a major port for all of Africa. Ships from all over the world arrive with goods to be delivered to all of Kenya and its landlocked neighbor, Uganda. The name "Mombasa" means The Island of War. It got this name from the many wars between the Africans, Arabs and Portuguese long ago. The Arabs have left a strong influence in Mombasa's Old Town, both in architecture and shipbuilding. The merchant sailors often wearing Asian turbans, bring figs, dates, dried fish, salt and carpets to Kenya through this port.

TRY THIS: Make a map of Kenya out of pizza crust. Add rhino, elephant and giraffe meat (pizza sausage). Top with grasses (shredded mozzarella) and red Lake Victoria water (tomato sauce). Bake in oven at 350 degrees for approximately 20-30 minutes.

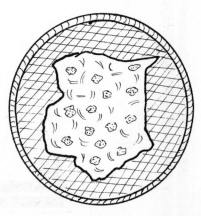

TRIBAL GROUPS OF KENYA

There are four large groups of people in Africa. They are Kikuyu, Luo, Luhya and Masai. The Masai belong to this last tribe. They are very tall and thin. They are herders that move with their animals in search of food. When they move on, they destroy their houses made of clay and cow dung. Traditionally, the Masai wore animal skins, but now make togas from sheets and blankets. The Masai will often hunt a lion using their handmade spears and shields. The shields are decorated with brightly colored designs. They are painted with paints made from clay. Clay red, white and black are the traditional colors. Today, more and more Masai are changing their ways of living in permanent homes, etc. How do you feel about this?

Should the Masai be forced to change their heritage? _____

TRY THIS: Design a Masai shield of your own. Color it in the traditional colors.

Masai

The Kikuyus live north of Nairobi in the area around Mt. Kenya. The mountain holds religious meaning for the people who believe their god, Ngai, lived on the mountaintop. The Kikuyus are good farmers and grow coffee, tea, and pyrethrum. Pyrethrum is used in insecticides. These people live in round houses and have small gardens. They also have herds of goats and sheep. Many Kikuyu now work in Nairobi's factories and stores.

Kikuyus

TRY THIS: Bake cookies in the shape of shields. Use any cutout cookie recipe. Frost the entire cookie first—half white, half red. Decorate with black icing in a decorator tube.

47

Color the costume on the left.
Design your own Kenyan costume
on the right. Color carefully. Try the
completed costume on the doll.

KENYA

Travelin' On ...

The following is a list of additional topics that interested or highly motivated students may want to learn more about:

Wild animals
Masai warriors
Mt. Kilimanjaro
The Arch Tree House
Serangetti Plains
British influences
Kenyatta
Mombasa
Coffee and tea production
Poaching
Native paintings
Swahili language
Artesian wells
Lungfish
Hyenas
Protected plants
Dr. Leakey
Prehistoric man
Olduvai Gorge

Quebec

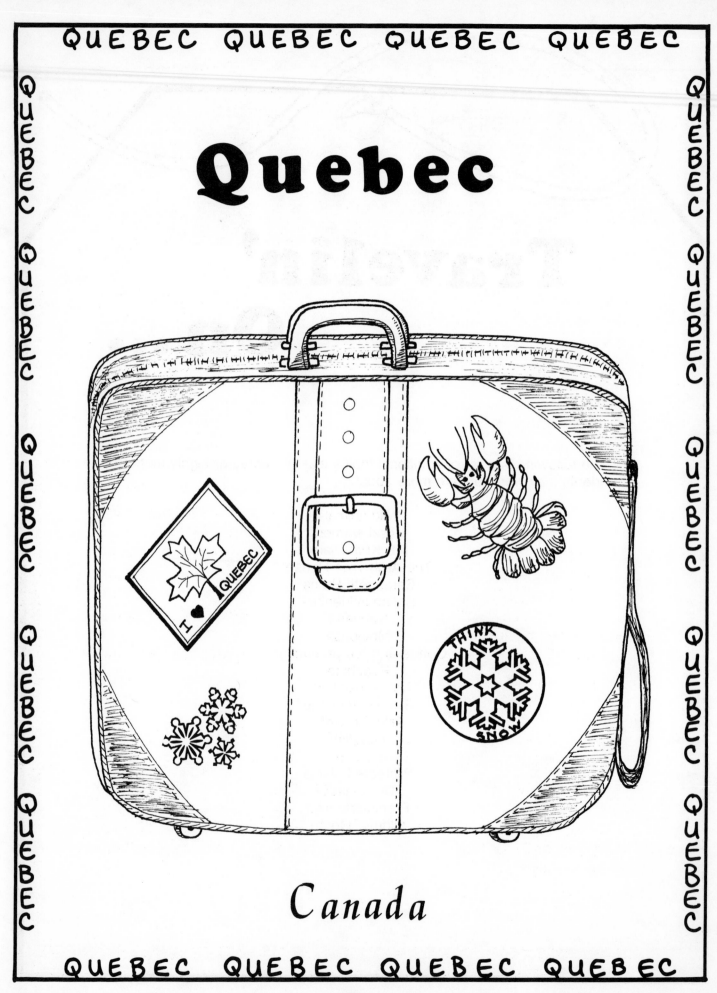

Canada

Tips for the Tour Guide

Explorers looked for a "Northwest Passage" to the Pacific. As they explored, they discovered many of Canada's great lands. Jacques Cartier explored and named the Gulf of St. Lawrence. He claimed the region for France. Samuel de Champlain explored the St. Lawrence River. He founded a colony and named it Quebec. It grew and prospered through the fur trade with the Indians. The Jesuit missionaries brought Christianity and expert record keeping to this new land. The French and English waged a struggle for the control over this new land. Eventually the struggle led to the French and Indian War of 1755 to 1763. The war ended with a great battle for Quebec. England won and took Quebec. The Treaty of Paris gave England all of Canada. The majority of colonists were French and kept their heritage alive.

The importance of the present-day St. Lawrence Seaway cannot be under told. Shipping to and from the Great Lakes is an important economic factor. Canada is rich in natural resources and has a strong production of nickel, aluminum, lead, copper, etc. Hydroelectric power is also an important source for the economy.

Although the Canadian national language is English, the French Canadians of Quebec still keep their native French language. Quebec City is the center of the Arts for Canada. Symphonies, art centers and theatres abound.

The wildlife of Quebec includes moose, bear, deer, bobcats, wolves, and many smaller animals. Birds, common and rare, are in abundance in Quebec. The tundra lands to the north provide their own stark beauty and abundant wildlife.

The city of Montreal hosted Expo '67. There a collection of international as well as future habitats were displayed. The theme was "Man and his World."

Quebec

CANADA

Locate:
★ Montreal
Quebec City

*

St. Lawrence Seaway
Hudson Bay
Atlantic Ocean
Gulf of St. Lawrence
Ontario
Maine
Newfoundland

CANADA

Provincial Coat of Arms

The coat of arms uses the emblems of France, Great Britain, and Canada. The three *fleur-de-lis* represent the three French Kings. The British lion appears in the center. The three maple leaves at the bottom represent Canada.

TRY THIS: Make a coat of arms for your family in the shield below.

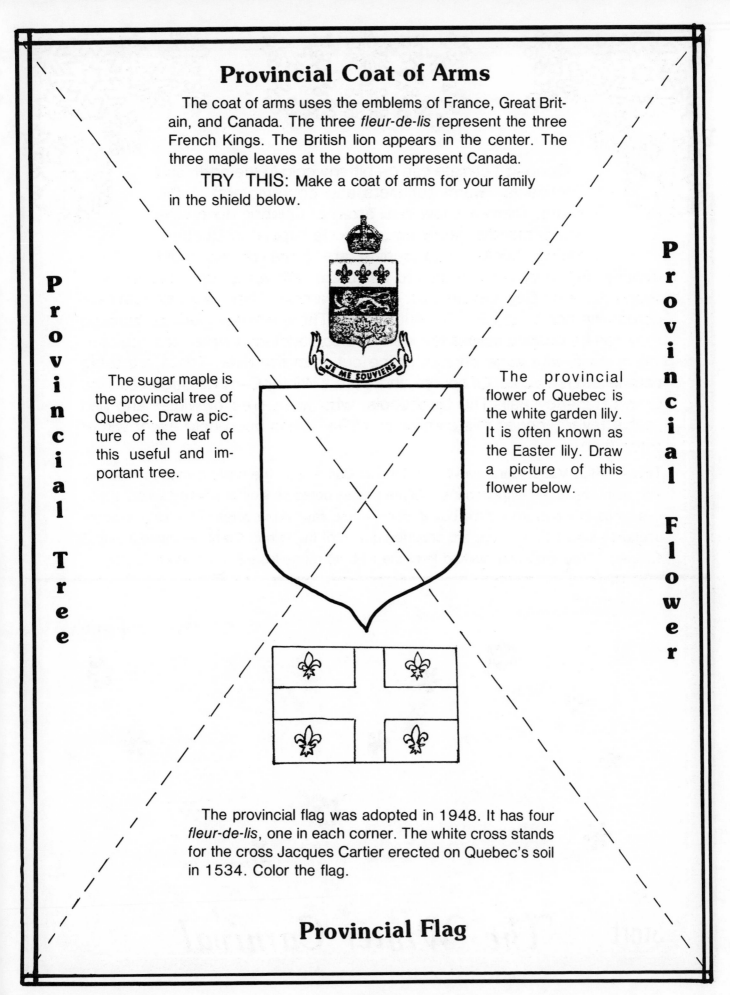

Provincial Tree

The sugar maple is the provincial tree of Quebec. Draw a picture of the leaf of this useful and important tree.

Provincial Flower

The provincial flower of Quebec is the white garden lily. It is often known as the Easter lily. Draw a picture of this flower below.

The provincial flag was adopted in 1948. It has four *fleur-de-lis*, one in each corner. The white cross stands for the cross Jacques Cartier erected on Quebec's soil in 1534. Color the flag.

Provincial Flag

Quebec's climate can be bitterly cold in the north and continental (warm summers and cold winters) in the south. There is snow in all areas of Quebec during the winter months. Many winter sports happen in Quebec. Skiing, hockey and curling are three of the most popular. February is the month to celebrate with winter carnivals in many towns. Quebec City has the most exciting carnival. There is an iceboat race across the half-frozen St. Lawrence River. The boats have skis on them so they can be pushed across the ice and also paddled in water. Ice sculpturing is done with huge chunks of ice cut from the river. There are a big parade and fireworks. Of course, there are a Winter Carnival Queen and the Grand Regency Ball. The Quebecois, who were tired of winter and had "cabin fever," began this carnival in 1894. It has been held every winter since then.

TRY THIS: Make your own Winter Carnival Game. Use the basic gameboard below. Add activities to the empty spaces. Game pieces could be skis or hockey sticks. If you use cards to move around the board, some could say "Sun comes out, must repair ice sculture—lose 1 turn," "You are crowned queen of the Winter Carnival—move ahead 3 spaces," "You are water soaked from the iceboat race—lose 2 turns warming up!"

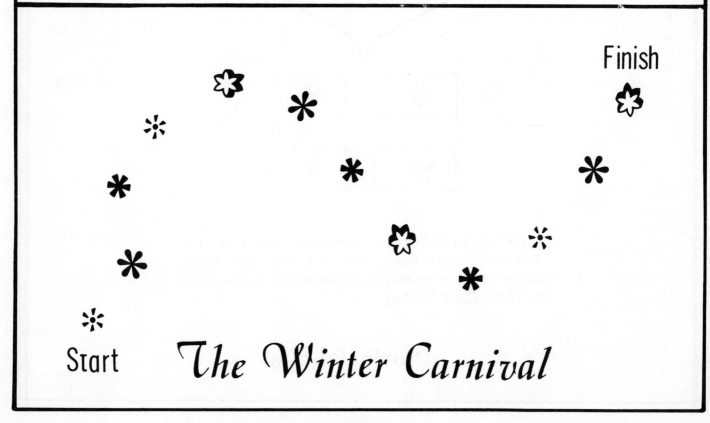

Finish

Start *The Winter Carnival*

54

Gaspé Peninsula

The rugged Gaspé Peninsula is a favorite area for artists, hikers and mountain climbers.

Bonaventure Island is one of the largest water bird refuges. More than 60,000 water birds nest on this island during the summer. Rare birds are protected here including the largest known colony of **gannets**.

Percé Rock, about 200 feet off the Gaspé coast rises straight off of the water to the height of 154-290 feet. This rock is 1565 feet long and 300 feet wide. Waves have eroded an arch over the years. At low tide, using a sandbar, some people cross from the little village of Percé to the famous rock. There are also cruises by boat that can be taken at any time of the day.

This peninsula is heavily wooded. Fishing villages lie along the northeast and eastern coast. Life in these villages is quite different from the busy city life of Montreal or Quebec. The hilly land keeps the people from traveling too far. The farmers and fishermen who live there are French Canadians. The families are large and work closely together to make a living. Some of the women still bake the famous bread that is baked in outdoor ovens and sold at roadsides. Life can be simple in Gaspe and there is a slow-paced feeling of peace.

TRY THIS: Try baking **French bread**. What is the trick to getting a crunchy crust? Research the rare **gannet birds**. What do they look like? How did they become so rare?

CHUBB CRATER

Chubb Crater is in northwestern Quebec. It can be located between Ungava Bay and Hudson Bay. It is the largest known meteor crater. This huge hole was discovered in 1950. It has the diameter of about 11,000 feet and the depth of 1350 feet.

TRY THIS: Make up an Indian legend about an Algonquin Indian tribe seeing the meteor falling from the sky. The Indians may have asked:

What have I done to have caused this?

Is this a sign of warning from the god of the stars?

Is this flaming ball alive?

Write your legend inside this crater below.

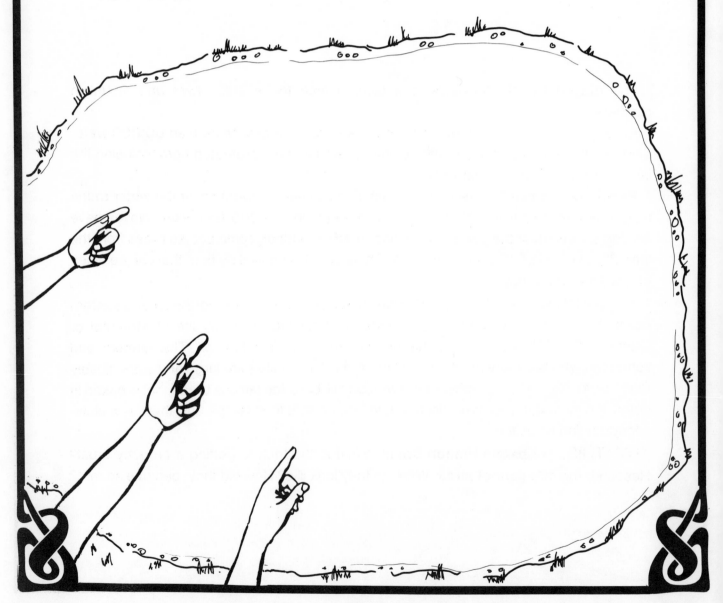

Quebec City

In 1534 Jacques Cartier explored the Gulf of St. Lawrence and landed on the Gaspé Peninsula. He called this new land "New France." Other explorers also searched for a water route across the top of the world.

Samuel de Champlain, often called "the father of Canada," came to New France. He started the first permanent settlement in Canada and called it Quebec. The settlement grew bigger and Champlain became the first governor. The Algonquin and Huron Indians were Champlain's friends. He helped them fight the Iroquois. They taught him how to use their canoes. They brought him furs and helped him explore. Champlain made excellent maps of the areas he explored.

The present city of Quebec is built on two levels: Upper Town and Lower Town. The two towns are connected by narrow, steep stairs and walkways. The streets have quaint French shops and stone homes. There are many beautiful churches. The Citadel overlooks the city from Upper Town. It was built in 1832. Prime Minister Churchill and U.S. President Franklin Roosevelt met in the Citadel to discuss World War II. Today it contains a museum and summer apartment for Canada's governor-general.

TRY THIS: Below are the names of several explorers who searched for a route across the top of the world. They discovered and mapped many famous sites in Canada. Try to find out more about these brave men and what they found.

Explorers   ## Discoveries

Eric the Red   _____

Sir Martin Frobisher (1576)   _____

Henry Hudson (1610)   _____

William Baffin (1616)   _____

John Davis   _____

John Cabot   _____

MAPLE SYRUP FESTIVAL

The production of maple syrup is greater in Quebec than any other North American area. During March, Plessisville celebrates the Maple Festival. Maple trees grow in this southern part of Quebec. They produce about 1,862,000 gallons of syrup which is made into sugar and taffy.

Sap usually begins to run on a bright, sunny morning after a cold, clear night. The wind is out of the west and temperatures are about 40 degrees. This poem can help you remember the influence of the wind:

When the wind is in the east,
The sap will run the least.
When the wind is in the west,
Then the sap will run the best!

The average maple tree runs 10-12 gallons of sap each season. This boils down to 1 gallon of syrup. In a bad year, when the sugar content is low, it may take 50 gallons of sap for 1 gallon of syrup.

The early Indians made "wax sugar" by dropping hot syrup from dippers onto the snow. They made cake or block sugar by boiling syrup without stirring and poured it into wooden molds. Some of the molds made maple sugar stars, moon, flowers and bears' paws for presents. No one knows exactly how Indians discovered maple syrup.

TRY THIS:
Write a story about how you think the Indians discovered maple syrup.

Try making and pulling taffy, using the following recipe:
3 cups sugar, ¼ tsp. salt, 1/8 tsp. soda, 3 tbsp. white Karo syrup, 1 cup water, 1 cup whipping cream.

Mix sugar, salt, soda, syrup and water in a large pan. Boil until mixture bubbles at 250 degrees. Slowly add whipping cream, a drop at a time. Do not stir this mixture while cooking. Boil at 260 degrees on a candy thermometer. Pour onto buttered platter or marble slab. Pull as soon as candy is cool enough to handle and is light in color. Cut into 1-inch pieces with scissors. Yield: 2-3 dozen pieces.

PLANT LIFE

The tundra land in northern Quebec cannot support trees because of the climate. The soil is always frozen below a few inches of topsoil. This topsoil is covered by great fields of moss and lichens. In the spring the colors are brilliant. During the fall, the colors become dull and gray. A great variety of flowering plants also grows in the tundra. These plants are able to grow, blossom, and produce seeds in only a few frost-free weeks.

Near the tree line, dwarf spruce trees grow. Going south, the trees and vegetation get larger and more varied.

Lumbering is a big industry. Quebec is the world's leading producer of pulp used for making newsprint.

The forests bloom in May with many wild flowers. The bellwort, bloodroot, dogtooth violets, spring beauties, squirrel corn and trilliums are a few varieties.

TRY THIS: Choose one of the wild flowers listed above that you have never before seen. Because plants are usually named for their unusual characteristics, draw a picture of your wild flower as you imagine in the first circle below. Then find a picture of the flower in a wild flower identification book. Draw the real flower in the second circle. Can you see why your plant got its name?_____

Lichens

Lumbering

Lilies

59

Apples

Quebec is one of North America's leading growers of apples. The Montreal area grows the most apples. There are nearly 10,000 different kinds of apples in the world. Apple growers only raise a few kinds. They have found the ones the buyers like the best.

TRY THIS: Find the names of these favorite apples in the apple search.

CORTLAND	DELICIOUS
GOLDEN	GRIMES
DELICIOUS	JONATHAN
WINESAP	NORTHERN SPY
	MCINTOSH
	ROME BEAUTY
	TRANSPARENT

GREENING	
WEALTHY	
STAYMAN	

and

```
A G W I N E S A P
J O N A T H A N I J K L
O M C I N T O S H T U S R
U S E N A M Y A T S A N C O
G O L D E N D E L I C I O U S
F S T N E R A P S N A R T A P
G N O R T H E R N S P Y O E
I N W G O S W E A L T H Y S
T W R O M E B E A U T Y E
L I D E L I C I O U S S
C O R T L A N D T R
A S G R I M E S
```

Asbestos

President
Quebec Asbestos Co.
Quebec, Canada

Dear Sir:

Sincerely,

Asbestos is a mineral that is found in large deposits in Quebec. It has fibers that are soft and bendable. They can be spun into thread and woven into cloth. The most remarkable quality of asbestos is that it is fireproof. It also does not conduct electricity.

Firemen's suits, gloves and helmets were made from asbestos. It has been used to insulate pipes, to line automobile brakes and can be mixed with paints. In recent years, it has been found that asbestos is a health hazard. The fine fibers can be breathed into the lungs. What do you suppose these findings have done to the asbestos industry in Quebec?

TRY THIS: Pretend you are an asbestos miner writing to the president of the Quebec Asbestos Company. State the reasons why you feel production of asbestos should continue or why it should be stopped.

Fishing

Fishing in the waters off of Quebec can include cod, herring and redfish. Crabs, lobsters and scallops are also found in offshore waters. The lakes and rivers are abundant with several kinds of trout including brook, gray and rainbow.

Lobsters and crabs are important products. The fishermen catch the lobsters in **pots**. Pots are wooden traps with funnel nets attached. When the lobster enters the net it cannot go back again—only into the pot. If more than one lobster gets into a pot, they fight and may break their claws.

TRY THIS: Draw a small picture of lobsters crawling into the pot.

and

The fur industry earns about $8,000,000 a year in Quebec. Trappers earn about $5,500,000 from beaver, fox, muskrat, marten and seal pelts. Mink are raised on farms. Mink ranchers earn about $2,500,000 a year. Animals are trapped during the coldest seasons because their fur is the thickest at that time.

Fur pelts were one of the main reasons the explorers settled in Canada. There was a great demand in Europe for fur coats and hats. Some Algonquin Indians still earn their living today hunting and fur trapping.

Fake fur coats and hats have become popular especially with wildlife protectors.

TRY THIS: Make a list of reasons why **real** fur is better. Make a list of reasons why **fake** fur is better.

Furs

SAINTE-ANNE-DE-BEAUPRÉ

In 1658 before Quebec was founded, some French sailors were caught in a storm in the St. Lawrence River. The winds were so violent that the sailors knew they would soon drown. They prayed to Sainte Anne for help and promised that if she would save them, they would build a shrine in her honor. It would be built in the most beautiful spot they could find. The story tells that the winds immediately died down and the sailors began to row away. Immediately the winds returned and blew their ship ashore. The shore they landed on appeared to be the most beautiful place in the world. It was a grassland covered with flowers. They named the site *Beau Pre* meaning "beautiful meadow." They built the shrine and soon all sailors on the St. Lawrence would stop to say a prayer to Sainte Anne. Miracles began to happen as the legend tells. Now, each year, millions of people visit the great shrine at Sainte-Anne-de-Beaupré.

TRY THIS: Make a multifold shrine to write this legend on. First fold a piece of 12" x 18" construction paper in half; then in half again. Cut the shrine shape, being careful to keep the sides attached. Open carefully. The four shrines could be glued into a triangular, standing shape by overlapping and gluing the two end shrines. Plan what you will say on the pages. What will you draw for pictures?

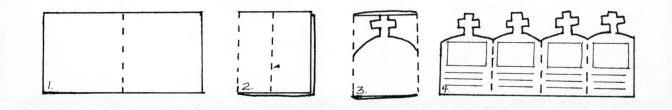

French Influences

The strong French influence in Quebec makes this an unusual province in Canada. The people speak French and keep their French traditions. About 90 percent of the people are Roman Catholic. Most of the private schools teach the Roman Catholic religion and the French language. The public schools use English as the basic language. The French Canadians feel so strongly about their heritage, they have even talked of seceding from Canada and making an independent state. When this idea was voted on, it failed by a large vote. Below are some French words to use for a calendar bulletin board. Learn a French word for a day.

Janvier	- January	Juillet	- July
Fevrier	- February	Août	- August
Mars	- March	Septembre	- September
Avril	- April	Octobre	- October
Mai	- May	Novembre	- November
Juin	- June	Decembre	- Décember

FRENCH WORD 1 — Word and Meaning Inside

Monthly Bulletin Board

Octobre

Language and Cooking

The **Quebecois**, French-speaking Canadians, love to eat and specialize in French cooking. Montreal is known for its many fine restaurants. Hearty pea soup with pork is the dish Quebec is known for. Pork is used in other favorite recipes. **Tourtiere**, a pork pie; **ragout de pattes**, pigs' feet stew; and **cretons**, cold pork slices, are a few of the special pork dishes.

Another favorite among French Canadians as well as Americans is the **crepe**. It can be used as a main dish or dessert. Below is a basic crepe recipe. A dessert filling and sauce are also given. Become a French chef for a day!

TRY THIS: Crepe mix. Follow directions on the box. Pour about 2 tbsp. of batter into a 6-inch skillet. Tilt from side to side to get batter all over bottom of pan. Do not turn. Invert pan and drop onto waxed paper.

Filling: Use a fruit-flavored yogurt. Spoon about 1 tbsp. in the middle of crepe and roll up.

Sauce: Thicken fruit, such as strawberries, with cornstarch. Spoon 2 tbsp. over the top of the crepe. Eat while still warm.

QUEBEC

CUT SLIT HERE

Color the costume on the left.

Design your own Quebec costume on the right. Color carefully. Try the completed costume on the doll.

64

Travelin' On ...

The following is a list of additional topics that interested or highly motivated students may want to learn more about:

Iroquois Indians
Algonquin Indians
Jacques Cartier
Huron Indians
Shipping on St. Lawrence Seaway
Building the St. Lawrence Seaway
French and Indian Wars
Treaty of Paris
Samuel de Champlain
Papermaking
Hydroelectric power
Gold mining
Lumbering
Fishing
Fur trapping
Naskapi Indians

Italy

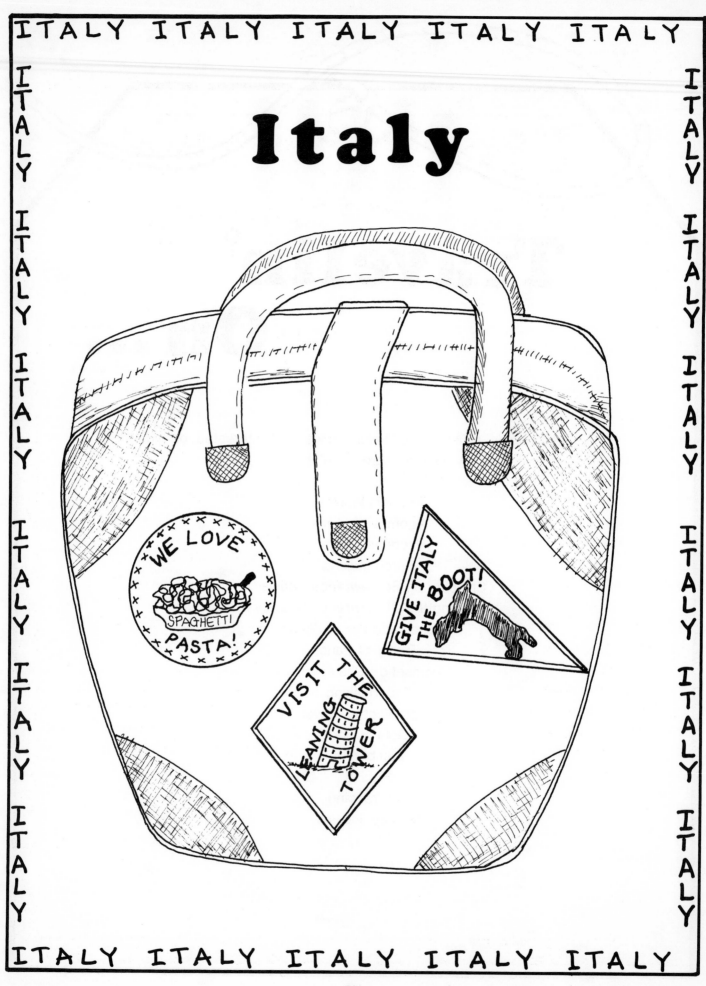

Tips for the Tour Guide

The official name is the Republic of Italy. It has approximately 57,000,000 people who are predominately Roman Catholic and speak Italian. The history of Italy and especially Rome is interesting and lengthy. It began about 2000 years ago in the lands surrounding the Mediterranean Sea. The area was called the Roman Empire. The ancient Romans built and invented many of today's conveniences. Before it became Italy around 1860, the country was divided into small city-states. The economy in Italy is enhanced by chemicals, fruit, grains, machinery, automobiles, olives, wine and tourism. The currency used in Italy is the lira.

Vatican City is an independent nation inside the city of Rome. It does have much influence over the education of the Italians because of their Roman Catholic beliefs.

Northern Italy has the most industry, farming and, consequently, wealth. The Italian government has formed an organization to help the people in southern Italy. There you would see stony farms, a dry climate and, consequently, poor people.

Every large and small city and town has a **piazza**, or square, where fun and activity go on. Around the square people may be sitting at sidewalk cafes, eating ice cream, drinking coffee or dancing with an accordion player. Everyone is welcome to join the fun in the evening.

Several of the most famous cities of Italy are Rome, the political capital; Milan, the financial capital; Turin, the industrial capital; Naples and Venice, tourist capitals; Genoa, the seafaring capital; Florence, the cultural capital; and Palermo, Sicily's capital.

Before leaving Rome, tourists must visit the Trevi Fountain. According to tradition, if they throw coins into the fountain, they will return someday.

The northern border of Italy is formed by the Alps. Italy also includes the island of Sicily in the Mediterranean Sea and Sardinia and Elba in the Tyrrhenian Sea.

Locate:
★ Rome
Naples
Turin
Milan
Venice
Palermo

Locate:
Sicily
Sardinia
Elba
France
Switzerland
Austria
Yugoslavia
Vatican City

ITALY

Locate:
Mediterranean Sea
Tyrrhenian Sea
Adriatic Sea
Ligurian Sea
Ionian Sea
Strait of Messina
Alps
Apennine Mts.

Italy is a **peninsula**. Why?

_____
_____

Mt. Etna and Mt. Vesuvius are two active volcanoes in Italy. Mt. Etna is on the island of Sicily and Mt. Vesuvius is near the city of Naples. Mt. Vesuvius erupted in 79 A.D. and buried the two cities of Pompeii and Herculaneum. They were buried under ashes and lava for many hundreds of years. Now they are uncovered and can be visited. Tourists stroll down the cobbled streets and look at the furniture and statues just as they were when the volcano erupted.

The United States also has an active volcano in Washington. It is Mt. St. Helens. Can you find out what happened to the surrounding area when it blew its top in 1980?

A diagram of the inside of a volcano is shown. Using a resource book, can you label the parts? You may want to explain what each part does.

V O L C A N O E S

a
b
c
d
e
f

THE STORY OF

One of the most famous legends telling about the birth of Rome tells of a woman named Silvia who was the niece of King Amulius. She gave birth to twin sons and named them Romulus and Remus. Because the King feared the boys would take over his kingdom, he ordered his servants to put the boys into a basket and float them down the Tiber River. They would surely die, he thought. But instead they landed on the banks of the river. A female wolf found them and raised them until they were taken in by a shepherd. The boys vowed that they would some day build a city on the Tiber River. It is said that Romulus built the beginnings of the city of Rome.

Rome is now the capital and most famous city in Italy. Rome has many treasures that help re-create the splendor of its history. One of the most famous ruins is the Colosseum. The Colosseum was finished in 80 A.D. There the Roman Emperors entertained the people with gladiators fighting to the death. During these early times, Rome had aqueducts that brought water to the people. At that time approximately one million people were being protected by police and fire fighters, also. The wealthy Romans' houses were heated and had running water. The public baths were also popular with the people. There they could take cold, warm and steam baths. The buildings also contained gymnasiums, libraries, stores and offices. These conveniences were truly luxuries!

During the sixth century, Rome began to lose its power. The ancient monuments began to crumble. The marble decorations were torn off the buildings and used to make lime. The water system of aqueducts fell apart and the city became a pasture for cattle. Later in the 1500's a restoration took place and many of the ancient treasures were restored.

During the early 1800's Napoleon Bonaparte and the Catholic Pope battled for control over the city. Finally, in 1929 a treaty was signed that created the state of Vatican City controlled by the Pope.

ROME

Today, Rome employs 250,000 people working for the Italian government. The city also houses 15,000 residents who are active in the Roman Catholic religion. The two most important industries in Rome are tourism and movie production. Moviemaking began in Rome in 1937 but World War II destroyed the growth of the industry. Again in the 1950's the movie industry took hold producing many fine movies. The Italian Westerns have become very popular and now Rome ranks among the leaders in moviemaking.

TRY THIS: The story of Romulus and Remus is a story handed down for many centuries. It tells how the city of Rome began. This is known as a **creation myth**. Can you create a legend about how your city began?

A Creation Myth about

_____

(YOUR CITY)

ITALIAN

Florence

Florence is known for its beautiful artwork and treasures. The night of November 4, 1966, was one of nightmares for the residents. The Arno River, which divides the city into two parts, flooded its banks and covered the city with a thick layer of water, mud and oil. All the valuable treasures were covered! Everyone in the town, rich and poor, worked together to save the paintings and sculptures. These workers became known as "Angels of the Mud." The National Library credits them for saving 4,000,000 valuable books. Today you can still see a dark line on some of the buildings noting the height of the water.

Locate the city of Pisa on a map. Have you ever heard of its famous leaning tower? This tower was built more than 800 years ago. After it was built, the land under it began to settle. Now it is leaning about five yards off center. The architects predicted it would fall shortly after it was built—but they were wrong, weren't they?

TRY THIS: Try building your own leaning building. Using toothpicks or blocks, have a contest to see who can build the tallest leaning building. You could also give prizes for the building that is most unusual, has the most details, and is tipped off center the farthest.

Pisa

CITIES

Genoa

Genoa is Italy's leading shipbuilding center. It also is known for soap production. Genoa's most famous resident was Christopher Columbus. The house in which he was born still remains.

Denim material used for making blue jeans was first made in Genoa. When you put on your jeans, you can call them "Genoas" instead!

TRY THIS: Design a pair of "Genoas" for yourself on the back of this sheet.

Venice was built by refugees running away from invaders in in 400 A.D. They hid in this city built on 100 islands near the Adriatic Sea. Being located so close to the sea, Venice became a maritime power as well as a wealthy city. The people of Venice were famous traders and brought back beautiful cloth of silk and brocade along with gold and spices. Famous painters were raised in Venice because they painted for the wealthy traders. There are now approximately 375,000 people living in Venice. Most live on the water and are connected to the mainland only by a railroad bridge and automobile road. The sea that brought the city wealth now is causing it problems. The buildings resting in the water are bring eaten away by the currents caused from boats and the seawater eroding the foundations. The city appears to be sinking about 12 inches every hundred years. Many expert engineers and architects are desperately trying to find a way to keep the city from being swallowed up by the sea!

Venice

ITALIAN

Long ago, two kinds of Latin were spoken in Italy. One kind was the language of the educated people and the other used by the common people.

Dante, the famous author, wrote a poem called **Divine Comedy.** He wrote it in the language of the common people because he wanted **all** of the Italian people to be able to read it. Because the poem was so popular, the common man's Latin became the official language of Italy.

Today there are still different dialects of Italian. People living on the island of Sicily may find it difficult to understand the people in Venice. Radio and television broadcasts are helping to reduce this communication problem.

TRY THIS: Below are some Italian phrases and words you may use if you were going to visit Italy.

Use some of these words to write a television commercial for a new kind of **pizza**!

cheese - formaggio	delicious - delizioso
good evening - buona sera	wine - vino
good - buona	yes - si
spaghetti - spaghetti	spice - spezie
thank you - grazie	tomato - pomodoro
child - bambino	crisp - croccante
restaurant - ristorante	crust - crosta
meat - carne	mushrooms - fungo
house - casa	bake - panet
vegetables - verdura	favorite - favorito
taste - gusto	

A Romance Language

Italian Pasta

Pizza, spaghetti and lasagna are all Italian foods that everyone loves!

Pizza is one of the main foods eaten by the people living in the poor areas in Southern Italy. It is inexpensive and simple to make, yet is tasty and good for you.

Spaghetti and lasagna are made up largely of **pasta**. It is estimated that there are at least one hundred different pasta shapes. They are divided into four categories: pasta for soup, for boiling, for stuffing and for baking. The names of pasta have colorful descriptions. Examples might be **agnolotti** meaning "little fat lambs," **cannelloni** meaning "big pipes," and **vermicelli** meaning "little worms." Luckily the pasta tastes better than it sounds! Spaghetti is probably the best known to the world.

TRY THIS: Have a Pasta Pig Out! Cook enough spaghetti for the number of people who entered the contest. Coat the spaghetti with butter to make it slippery. The winner must finish all of the spaghetti using only his mouth!

It might also be fun to have a contest to design a mechanical spaghetti fork. The fork would be used to maneuver the slippery, long spaghetti to the hungry, waiting mouths.

You may also decide to find out if there really are one hundred different kinds of pasta. List all the ones you can find in the grocery store. You may have a pasta specialty food shop near you. Put the names in alphabetical order. This could be the beginning of an Italian cookbook.

Mechanical Fork

Christmas

Each year the Italians celebrate Christmas with decorated trees and gift exchanges. There are several different kinds of Christmas customs in different parts of Italy. In some homes a big dinner with twenty-four different meatless dishes is served. Then people go to the Midnight Mass on Christmas Eve. Some people burn a yule log in their fireplaces as the children open small gifts. Most homes do have a **presepio** or manger scene. It may contain as many as one hundred statues which recall the scene of Jesus' birth. January 6 is also a traditionally special day in many parts of Italy. **Befana**, a little old lady, brings gifts to the children as she tried to do when Jesus was born. She never found Jesus, but the children of Italy receive her presents every year.

TRY THIS: On the back of this sheet, draw a picture of what you think Befana looks like as she delivers gifts to the Italian children.

Many of our customs and celebrations have stayed the same as in Roman times.

Valentine's Day is a modern festival that dates back to old Rome. The first festival was a party thanking the Roman god Lupercus for keeping the wolves moved away, but the celebration continued. Young men drew the names of young ladies to see who their sweethearts would be for that year. February 15 became a "Festival of Love" day. Then Christianity came to Rome and people were thrown into prison or to the lions for no longer believing in the Roman gods. The Emperor at that time felt soldiers should not marry because they would not want to go away to war if they had wives. Valentine, a priest, married the soldiers secretly. He became a saint known as St. Valentine. He was put into jail. Children would throw flowers and love notes to him. St. Valentine died on February 14. This is the date we now celebrate St. Valentine's Day. The god associated with this special day is Cupid, the Roman god of love.

TRY THIS: Practice writing Valentine "puns." Examples would be "I'll go 'hog' wild over you," "I'm 'ape' for you," and "Let's make beautiful music together." Design a valentine using your favorite pun.

St. Valentine's Day

FAST, FIERY,

The city of Turin in northwestern Italy is its industrial capital. The largest of its 20,000 factories is FIAT. It is the fourth largest automobile producer in the world. It is privately owned. The initials FIAT stand for Febbrica Italiana Automobili Torino. The FIAT company built almost a small city for its workers. It provides a recreation building for children, a church, nursery, medical center and supermarket.

The FIAT is a small car and popular in Italy. It fits the narrow, winding streets and does not use much gasoline.

Italy also produces some of the best racing and sports cars in the world. Have you ever heard of **Lamborghini**, **Ferrari**, **Alfa Romeo**, **Lancia** or **Maserati**?

One of the fastest cars in the world is the Ferrari. It was first built by the Italian Enzo Ferrari. His racing cars are always bright red and have the Ferrari symbol of the galloping horse painted on them. In the factory today only 2000 cars are made each year. They cost about 40 to 60 thousand dollars each!

TRY THIS: Try to design a car like Enzo Ferrari would have. Make it low and sleek for speed! What color would you paint it? _____
Draw your company's logo in the circle below.

Carlo Lorenini used the pen name of Carlo Collodi when he wrote his most famous book, **The Adventures of Pinocchio**. The story has been translated into several languages. Carlo was born in Florence, Italy, and is one of its most famous authors.

The story of Pinocchio is about a wooden puppet who wants to become a real boy. Read the famous story again and try to picture Pinocchio as an animal. Choose any real or imaginary animal. Decide what part of the animal will change shape, and then write a short adventure to fit into the beginning and ending of the story below.

Once upon a time in the sleepy town of _____ (name) lived the animal _____ (name of animal) and his keeper. _____ (animal's name) was very bored and sad. He watched all the neighborhood kids playing and having fun together. If only he could, too!

One dark, crisp night _____
_____
_____.

Wow! That was close! _____ (animal's name) decided that it was good being a _____ (kind of animal)! He hurried home and lived happily ever after in the sleepy and less boring town of _____ (town's name).

Perhaps you'll want to make a marionette of your animal. Cut the pattern pieces out of wood or double corrugated cardboard. Use screw eyes and hooks to connect. Attach clear filament line to parts you want to move. Make a crossbar to maneuver the strings. Add your own tail, ears, eyes, nose and mouth. There may be other animal parts and details that you need for your story.

CARLO COLLODI

Popular People

Each one of the people listed below is Italian. They are famous not only in Italy, but all over the world. Some lived long ago and some are still alive today.

Next to the person's name, write at least two things that made this person famous. You may need to use an encyclopedia or other reference book for clues.

Then use the pattern below to make twenty cards. Write the famous person's name on the left side of the rectangle. On the right, list why he is famous. Cut each card apart in a different way so the two pieces can be matched together later. (No pairs should be alike.)

TRY THIS: Now, try to match the cards! After **you** have mastered it, try your game on a friend. Time yourselves to see who can match the pairs the fastest.

Julius Caesar	1._____	2._____
Enrico Caruso	1._____	2._____
Christopher Columbus	1._____	2._____
Leonardo da Vinci	1._____	2._____
Lorenzo de Medici	1._____	2._____
Federico Fellini	1._____	2._____
Enzo Ferrari	1._____	2._____
Galileo	1._____	2._____
Luigi Galvani	1._____	2._____
Giuseppe Garibaldi	1._____	2._____
Gina Lollobrigida	1._____	2._____
Sophia Loren	1._____	2._____
Guglielmo Marconi	1._____	2._____
Michelangelo	1._____	2._____
Marco Polo	1._____	2._____
Sylvester Stallone	1._____	2._____
Antonio Stradivari	1._____	2._____
Amerigo Vespucci	1._____	2._____
Alessandro Volta	1._____	2._____
Your choice	1._____	2._____

Italy

Color the costume on the left.
Design your own Italian costume on the right. Color carefully. Try the completed costume on the doll.

Travelin' On ...

The following is a list of additional topics that interested or highly motivated students may want to learn more about:

Sicily
Capri
Michelangelo
Marble
Soffioni-Natural Steam
Circus Maximus
Wine production
Famous artists, sculpturers
Education
Vatican City
Hannibal
Napoleon Bonaparte
Scirocco winds
Mt. Etna
Sports
Sardinia
Milan shopping centers
Christopher Columbus
Museums
Ferragosto holiday
Easter celebration
Marzipan
Sagra della Brociola
Hospitality Fair
Partita a Scacchi
Palio horse race
Opera
Olives
Roman gods and myths
Trevi Fountain

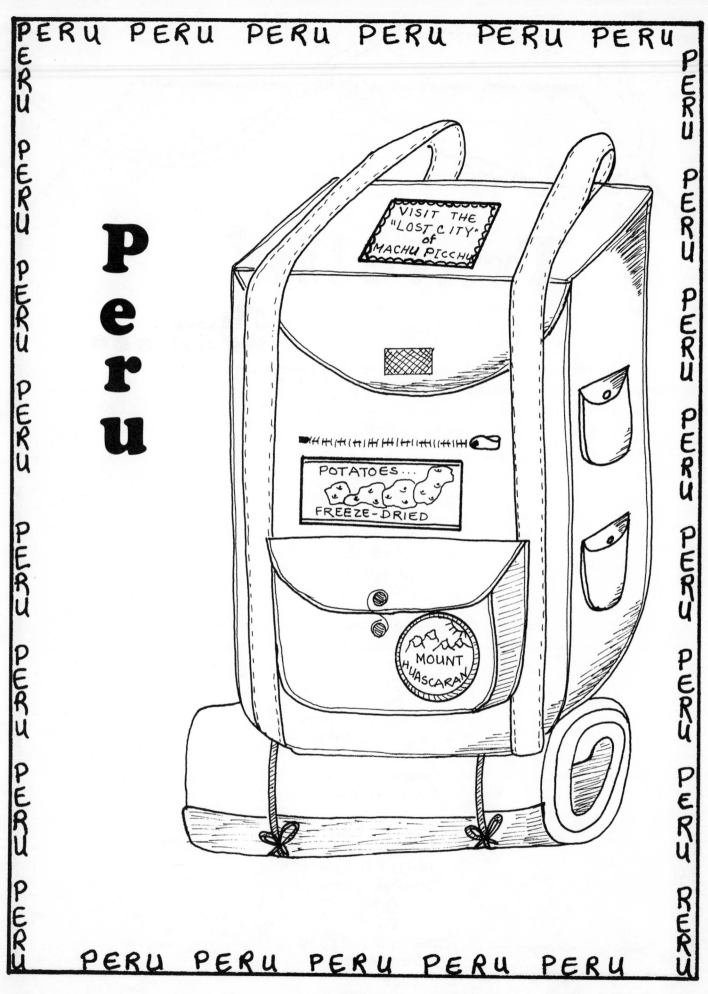

Tips for the Tour Guide

The country of Peru has a population estimated at 13,000,000. Most of this population lives high in the Andes Mountain range. Most of these people are herders and farmers. The high altitude affects the climate dramatically even though Peru is located very near the equator. The coastal area on the west side of the country has great potential for growth and wealth. Petroleum, fishing and culture are being developed in this area. The capital city of Lima is also located there. As the people come out of the mountains to the cities, the problems begin to arise there. Language is a barrier as is the lack of education and skills for city employment. Slums are a great concern to the government.

The country does export minerals, fish meal, cotton, sugar and coffee. The lumber industry is also improving. Chief agricultural products are cotton, sugar, wool, hides, coffee and rice. Most of the farmers in the highlands are most concerned with keeping their own families supplied with food.

The Inca civilization was a very highly developed culture. It had better systems of communication and transportation than the present day Peruvians have. The city of Machu Picchu was the cultural center of the Incas. It was hidden by jungle growth until 1911 when it was discovered by an American archeologist.

The people celebrate holidays in much the same way as most people—parties of food and dancing. Other entertainment includes relaxing on the beaches, bullfighting, cockfights, soccer (futbol), golf, tennis, polo and mountain climbing.

The Spanish conquered Peru in 1533. The Peruvians were not prepared for war and the country fell easily. Independence was finally gained in 1821. Peru was the last Spanish colony to gain independence.

Locate:
- Amazon River
- Andes Mountains
- Atlantic Ocean
- Pacific Ocean
- Equator

Color:
- Sierra Highlands (Orange)
- Montaña Jungle (Green)
- Coast Desert (Brown)

Locate Cities:
1. Li _ _
2. Ar _ _ _ _ _ _ _
3. Mac _ _ P _ _ _ _ _ _
4. Iq _ _ _ _ _ _
5. Pi _ _ _
6. Tru _ _ _ _ _ _

PERUVIAN PAPAS

The ancestors of the Incas were the first people to raise potatoes. Before 6000 B.C. the Indians of Peru collected wild potatoes. It soon became the most important food in their diet. The potato, or **papa** as it is called, was not only eaten, but also the potato spirits were worshipped and used in their arts.

Farmers may grow as many as 3000—5000 different varieties of potatoes. Many do not resemble our mind's picture of a potato. They come in all colors, shapes and sizes. Many look like tiny pineapples, some like coral snakes, others like bright red cherries and some like purple gumdrops. Each kind has a name often creative and very funny. In Quechua (KECH-wa), the native language, a long flat potato is called **mishipasinghan,** which means "cat's nose." A knobby, hard-to-cook potato is called **lumchipamundana,** which means "potato which makes young bride weep."

The Peruvian Indians were the first to make freeze-dried potatoes called **chuño.** During the coldest nights in the Andes Mountains, small, bitter potatoes are spread on the ground to freeze. The next day the sun dries them. After several days and nights of freezing and drying, they are gathered into small piles. The villagers rhythmically stomp on them with their bare feet. Then the potatoes are soaked in the water for three weeks and again dried. After this process, the chuño will keep up to four years.

In prehistoric times, chuño was placed in the tombs of the dead as food for their journey to the afterworld.

Draw a strange shape in each of the bushel baskets below. Give your paper to a friend to name each shape. These could be new varieties of potatoes you have created!

THE INCA

The Inca Indians were the first people in South America. At the height of their civilization, their population numbered about 7 million people. The civilization had well-organized armies, good communications and strong social and political systems.

The capital was at Cusco. It is about 11,000 feet above sea level. Cusco had many palaces and government buildings. The Temple of the Sun shone with gold and precious stones.

Inca society had four classes: the ruling class, the nobility, the common people and the slaves. The way people lived depended on which class they belonged to.

The foods of the Peruvians today are similar to the food of the ancient Incas. The most staple food was the potato. Meat consisted of llama and guinea pig. Corn, beans, squash and tomatoes were also part of the diet.

The men wore short shirts and tunics. Their hair was braided and worn like a turban. Women wore long dresses wound around the waist with a sash. Depending on the class, the jewelry worn could be every elaborate and expensive or very quaint.

The Inca religion consisted of the powerful Sun god, Viracocha, and his assistants, the moon, thunder, weather, stars, etc.

The Inca craftsmen produced large quantities of pottery, all similarly designed. Metal workers made jewelry, tools and weapons from silver, copper, gold and bronze. Perhaps the most famous work was one by stone workers. They were able to fit stones together so carefully that a knife blade could not be slipped between. Many of the Inca buildings that can be viewed today are still in very good condition. Stones weighing many tons were brought to building sites using rollers, inclined planes, wedges and ropes.

EMPIRE

A

B

The Incas were an agricultural community. They kept all of the crops in storehouses and saved them for distribution to each family.

The roads and mail service were superb. The roads were paved with flat stones and retaining walls. Bridges and rest stations were built where needed. Runners were the mail service and could deliver a message at the rate of 150 miles per day.

The Incas did not develop a true system for writing. They did work out a number system of knotted strings. The system is called **quipu** (KEE-poo). From the main cord hung smaller strings of different colors. There were groups of knots tied at different lengths.

C

Part of the costumes worn by the Incas at special ceremonies was the elaborate headpieces worn by the men. Using one of the two designs (C), make a headpiece using colored paper, silver and gold wrapping paper, etc. Make a simple hat frame of strips of construction paper (A,B). Add the design to the front (D).

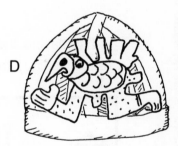

D

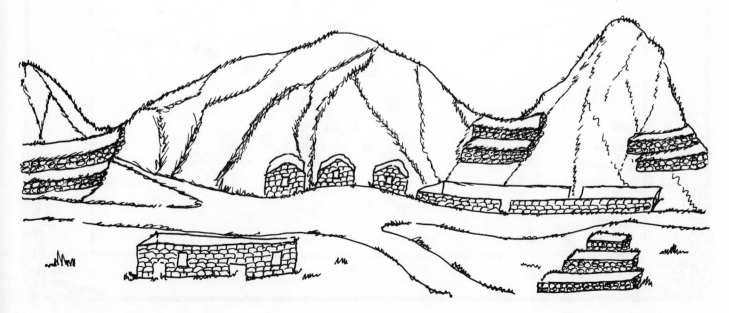

Precious Metals

Many hundreds of years ago Spanish rulers searched for gold and silver. In recent years other minerals have become important resources. These minerals include iron, copper, lead, coal, zinc and petroleum.

In 1533 the Spanish, who had taken over the Incas, captured the Inca ruler and held him for ransom. It was perhaps the greatest ransom in history—a room full of gold and silver! Unfortunately the Spaniards did not keep their bargain and killed the ruler and took the ransom, too.

While the Spanish continued to rule Peru, they sent gold and silver to Spain. Of course, the king claimed "his royal fifth." The ships carrying this precious cargo were not always delivered. Pirates often attacked the ships and took the cargo.

and
Pirates

Try playing the board game below. Roll a die for your moves. The first ship to reach Spain is the winner.

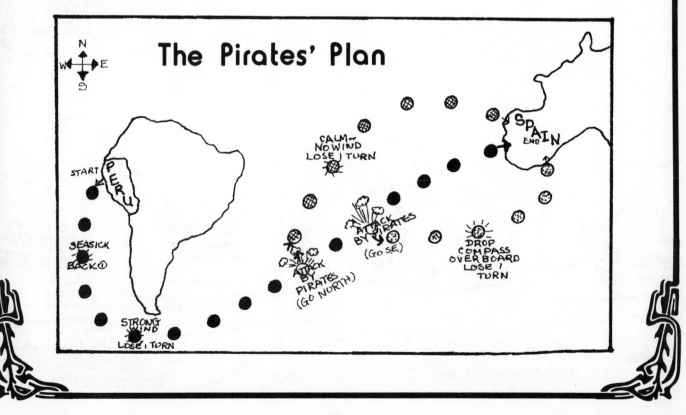

ANIMALS OF THE ANDES

The alpacas and llamas are raised by the Peruvians for their soft, thick wool. The alpaca's coat can grow so long that it touches the ground. The wool is sheared from the animals and sometimes dyed and woven into fabric. This fabric, called alpaca, sheds the rain and snow!

Colorful tassels dangle from the ears of the llamas. These tassels show who owns the animal.

Guanacos, members of the camel family, are found from the coast to the mountains in Peru.

Vicuna are only found in a few areas high in the Andes Mountains. They have been hunted for their wool and now the numbers are dwindling. Many years ago only very important people were allowed to wear clothing made of vicuna wool.

Cut off the bottom of this paper. Cut out the circle carefully so you can have a peephole inside your folded card. Use the circle as part of a Peruvian picture. (Eye on a face, pancake hat, potato, etc.). Inside the picture should be of a llama, alpaca, guanaco or vicuna. Write several complete sentences about the animal you have drawn. Be sure to give it a name.

PERUVIAN

Music is an important part of every festival. CONJUNTOS, or native bands, play at every party. Most of the native songs are played on a 5-tone, or pentatonic scale. Many different instruments are used to give variety to the sound. Some of the instruments are the ANTARA, or panpipes; the QUENA, or small flute; PINCULLO, or whistle; TINYA, or small drum, and other stringed instruments such as the HARP, VIOLIN and GUITAR.

The songs and dances help celebrate the OCTOBER FAIR. This celebration began when a wall remained standing after an earthquake in Lima in 1746. This wall has a famous religious painting on it.

Peruvian PEASANT DAY is celebrated on June 24th to praise the farmers. November second is ALL SOUL'S DAY. People visit the cemeteries and bring flowers and food for the dead.

CHRISTMAS is also celebrated everywhere.

Fiesta days are a change from the daily pattern of hard work for the Peruvians. Fiestas are the main recreation of the people. They wear their brightest costumes, dance and drink native beer made from corn.

Try to find the twelve musical instruments and holiday names in this word search.

See if you can draw a picture of a fiesta. Include a band with all of the musicians. Bright costumes are important to the dancers.

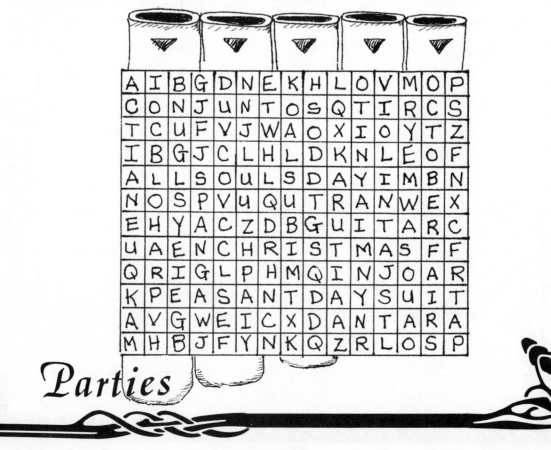

A	I	B	G	D	N	E	K	H	L	O	V	M	O	P
C	O	N	J	U	N	T	O	S	Q	T	I	R	C	S
T	C	U	F	Y	J	W	A	O	X	I	O	Y	T	Z
I	B	G	J	C	L	H	L	D	K	N	L	É	O	F
A	L	L	S	O	U	L	S	D	A	Y	I	M	B	N
N	O	S	P	V	U	Q	U	T	R	A	N	W	E	X
E	H	Y	A	C	Z	D	B	G	U	I	T	A	R	C
U	A	E	N	C	H	R	I	S	T	M	A	S	F	F
Q	R	I	G	L	P	H	M	Q	I	N	J	O	A	R
K	P	E	A	S	A	N	T	D	A	Y	S	U	I	T
A	V	G	W	E	I	C	X	D	A	N	T	A	R	A
M	H	B	J	F	Y	N	K	Q	Z	R	L	O	S	P

Parties

The east side of the Andes jungles and the plains make up the **mon-taña**. The area is isolated with few roads and only the rivers are used for transportation. It is an underdeveloped region with large jungles. Half of the total area of Peru is part of the montaña. The soil is very rich and holds much moisture. The climate is hot and humid with heavy downpours from December through April. Because of this climate, the area is not heavily settled. There are a few Peruvian Indian tribes in the back country. These climatic conditions are excellent for growing rice, fruits and vegetables. Unfortunately, with the poor transportation system, the foods cannot be delivered to the big cities along the coast. Therefore, this rich jungle area goes undeveloped.

Iquitos, with a population of 1,000,000 is the main city of the montaña jungle region. Iquitos is located on the Amazon River, which is the reason for its importance. This city is the only lifeline with the outside world. Products exported from the port are lumber, **leche caspi** (chewing gum base), animal hides, alligator skins and plants used for medicine and dye.

Like most of the Amazon jungle, the birds and butterflies have wings of brilliant colors. Often the birds are sold to pet shops in large cities in Peru. The insects are also sold, but usually have been killed and mounted to show off the beautiful iridescent blues and other bright colors.

Use the pattern on this page or one of your own. Try making a jungle butterfly, remembering that these delicate insects are symmetrical.

Tear small pieces of construction paper to fill in the designs on the insect. The pieces should overlap. Don't forget the antennae.

Montaña » Jungles

Sierras

Three ranges of mountains make up the Andes Mountains in the highlands or SIERRAS. These mountain ranges make up more than one-third of the entire area of Peru. Over half of the people of Peru live in the Sierra region. Most of them are herders and farmers. The climate can range from moderate to FRIGID. The elevation has much influence on the climate. During the rainy season, the mountain rivers swell and overflow, taking mud with them. These mud slides, called HUAYCOS, have been known to bury entire villages.

Llamas, vicuna and alpacas live in the pastures of these high mountains.

The farmers, CAMPESINOS, live in little mud or stone huts and farm a small piece of land. They grow potatoes, corn, grain, beans and raise a few cattle. Their main concern is to have food for themselves to eat.

Altitude sickness, SOROCHE, is not known to the highland Peruvians. The air is very thin, but the natives seem able to work even in these conditions.

The highland Peruvians have kept the traditional dress of the past. Their clothing is multicolored and bright against the mountain scenery, often covered with everlasting snow. The women wear large, full, earth-sweeping skirts and felt hats shaped like upside-down PANCAKES. These hats often tell what part of Peru the woman came from. Shawls are not only used to keep warm, but also to carry a load of corn or wool. The men wear the unusual hat called CHULLO. It is also multicolored and has ear flaps. A PONCHO is worn for warmth and to keep off the rain. The children dress as their parents do.

DOWN
1. Mud slides
2. Cape or sleeveless jacket
3. Hat with ear flaps
4. Very cold

ACROSS
2. Shape of ladies' hats
5. Highland farmers
6. Altitude sickness
7. Highlands

On the back of this paper, draw a picture of **your** family dressed in native Peruvian costumes.

ANDES HIGHLANDS

Coastline of Peru

The narrow strip of land between the Pacific Ocean and the west side of the Andes Mountains is Peru's wealthiest area. Its ocean seaports, the capital city of Lima, petroleum fields, fishing industry and the center of culture are all located in this narrow piece of land stretching the length of Peru.

This coastal area is largely desert and may not have any rain at all for an entire year. A system of irrigation makes this area the most productive agricultural area. Even though Peru is very close to the equator, the climate is cool and damp because of the Peru Current. During the months of June to October, the winds blow the warm surface waters away from the coast, and this causes the cooler waters from below to come to the surface. This season is winter. The sun is rarely seen because of a cloud that covers it and produces a fine drizzle each day.

The Peru Current is considered a valuable resource because it may be the richest source of ocean food in the world. One of the most important fishes to Peruvians is the anchovy. Ground anchovy is used in poultry food. It is also the chief food of many sea birds.

PERU CURRENT

1. What makes the coastal area, Peru's richest area?

_____, _____, _____, _____

2. What kind of climatic region occurs along the coast? _____
   a. jungle   b. mountain highland   c. desert

3. What changes the climate along the coast? _____

4. Why is the Peru Current important to the coast?

_____

5. Why is the anchovy important to the Peruvians?

_____

6. Try to find out what an anchovy looks like and what it is used for.

_____

Desert

Color the costume on the left.

Design your own Peruvian costume on the right. Color carefully. Try the completed costume on the doll.

PERU

Travelin' On ...

The following is a list of additional topics that interested or highly motivated students may want to learn more about:

Education
Quechua
Spanish Conquest
Alpaca fur
Gold
Potatoes
Jungle birds
Jungle animals
Peru Current
Religions
Foods
Volcanoes
Chewing gum
Machu Picchu
Gunpowder
Lima
Inca treasures
Amazon River
Weather
Guanaco
Vicuna
Mahogany
Lake Titicaca
Earthquake belt
Monetary Unit: sol
Altitude sickness
Native dances
Bullfighting
Sports
Guano

India

Tips for the Tour Guide

More than 600 million people of India live in a land one-third the size of the United States. There are fourteen main languages and more than seven hundred other languages and dialects.

The caste system is still followed in some places although it has been forbidden by the government.

Most families live in small villages in mud huts with little furniture. There are extended families working together in rice or wheat fields. Work is hard and after the family is fed, there is usually not much left to sell.

Hinduism is the main religion with four out of five Indians. This religion regards cows as sacred and forbids the eating of beef. The cattle are milked but never killed. They often eat the precious food crops of the poor families.

Cities in India are highly populated. They are the centers of industry, commerce and transportation.

The British influence remains from when India was her colony. Independence came in 1947 and with independence came new problems.

The Ganges River north of Calcutta is sacred to many Hindus. There the people drink, bathe, worship and scatter the ashes of their dead, hoping for reincarnation.

One of the major problems of the people of India is its overpopulation. Since the advancement of medicines and public health measures, the death rate has dropped. Every two years India adds 25 million people to its numbers. This only enhances the continuing problem of rural poverty. Economic growth is slow and schooling needs to be provided for millions of children. Technical jobs are also needed for the trained.

Although there are many remaining problems, India has great hopes for the future. They are willing to make sacrifices for their democratic form of government. The benefits will come soon—they hope.

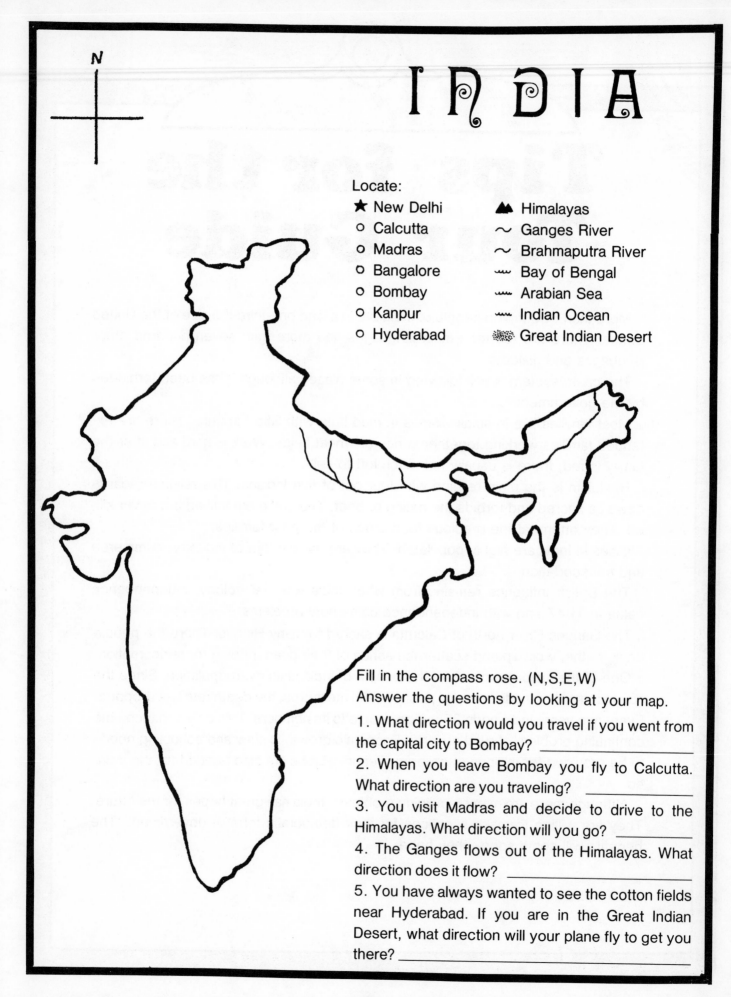

I N D I A

N

Locate:

★ New Delhi   ▲▲ Himalayas
○ Calcutta   ～ Ganges River
○ Madras   ～ Brahmaputra River
○ Bangalore   ⌇ Bay of Bengal
○ Bombay   ⌇ Arabian Sea
○ Kanpur   ⌇ Indian Ocean
○ Hyderabad   ▒ Great Indian Desert

Fill in the compass rose. (N,S,E,W)
Answer the questions by looking at your map.

1. What direction would you travel if you went from the capital city to Bombay? _____

2. When you leave Bombay you fly to Calcutta. What direction are you traveling? _____

3. You visit Madras and decide to drive to the Himalayas. What direction will you go? _____

4. The Ganges flows out of the Himalayas. What direction does it flow? _____

5. You have always wanted to see the cotton fields near Hyderabad. If you are in the Great Indian Desert, what direction will your plane fly to get you there? _____

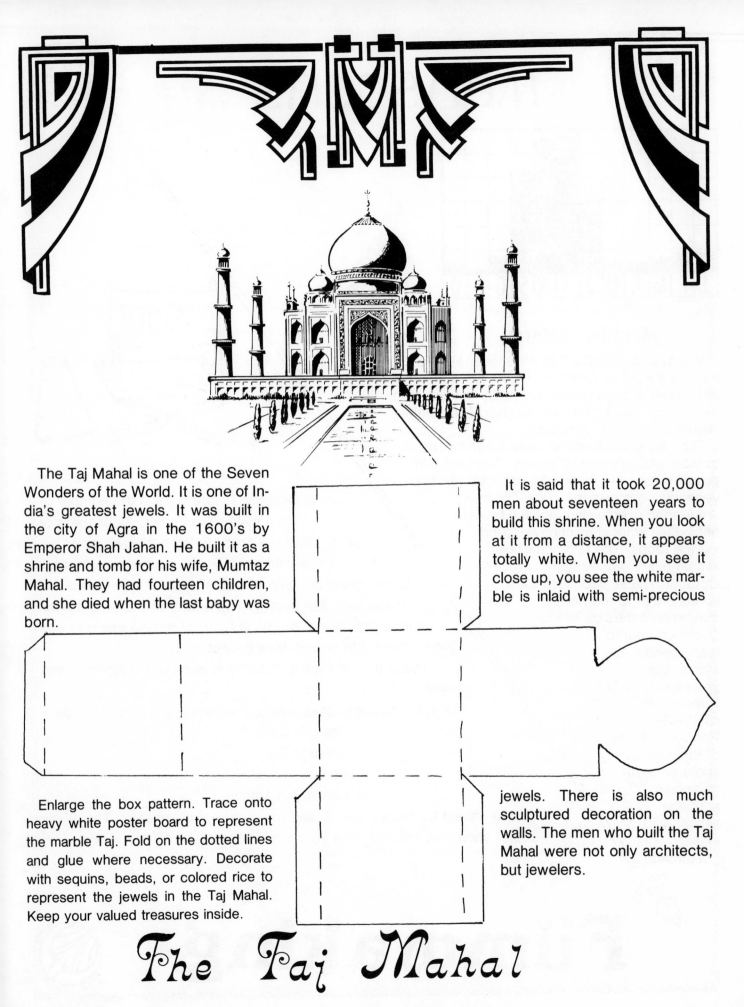

The Taj Mahal is one of the Seven Wonders of the World. It is one of India's greatest jewels. It was built in the city of Agra in the 1600's by Emperor Shah Jahan. He built it as a shrine and tomb for his wife, Mumtaz Mahal. They had fourteen children, and she died when the last baby was born.

It is said that it took 20,000 men about seventeen years to build this shrine. When you look at it from a distance, it appears totally white. When you see it close up, you see the white marble is inlaid with semi-precious

Enlarge the box pattern. Trace onto heavy white poster board to represent the marble Taj. Fold on the dotted lines and glue where necessary. Decorate with sequins, beads, or colored rice to represent the jewels in the Taj Mahal. Keep your valued treasures inside.

jewels. There is also much sculptured decoration on the walls. The men who built the Taj Mahal were not only architects, but jewelers.

The Taj Mahal

MONSOONS

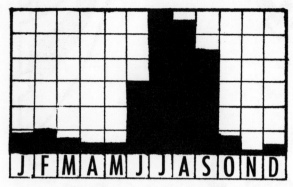

J F M A M J J A S O N D

Monthly Rainfall

March to June is the hot, dry season in India. Soil becomes hard as rock and vegetation withers and dies. Dust is blown everywhere by the hot, summer winds. The nights are also hot. The weather makes people feel very tired.

Then toward the end of June black clouds, thunder and lightning fill the sky. Soon the rain **pours** out of the skies. Almost instantly the vegetation comes back to life. The rivers are filled to overflowing, and the farmers begin their work of planting and tending the crops. The rains continue almost every day through October. The monsoon rains are so important to the people that, should they be late or a little off-course, many people may starve. Can you explain WHY? Cherrapunji (CHEHR-uh-Poon-jee) is one of the wettest spots on earth. Its annual rainfall is almost 450 inches (1100cm).

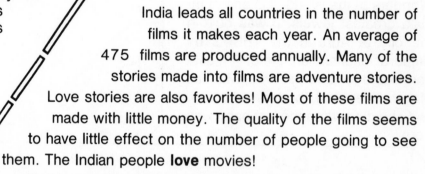

India leads all countries in the number of films it makes each year. An average of 475 films are produced annually. Many of the stories made into films are adventure stories. Love stories are also favorites! Most of these films are made with little money. The quality of the films seems to have little effect on the number of people going to see them. The Indian people **love** movies!

Today the filmmaking industry is centered in Bombay and Madras.

On the next page, draw a poster advertising a new film called:

Crisis in Calcutta

Calcutta Cutie

Bombs over Bombay

Mystery in Madras

The title should be printed clearly and the picture drawn neatly. The whole poster should be colorful. Use your imagination!

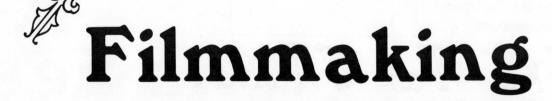

Filmmaking

MUSIC

There are many differences in the music of northern India and southern India. Two characteristics are the same in both areas: the **raga**, which is the melody, and the **tala**, which is the rhythm.

In recent years there has been a strong interest in music and dance that focuses on modern living and influences from other countries. Folk music, dance and drama have gained popularity along with dance, radio and television.

Traditional Indian instruments, such as the sitar, are played with classical music. Only the wealthy people have these opportunities.

Movies

ANIMALS

Foothills

There is a huge variety of animal life in India. In the **foothills** of the Himalayan Mountains, the villagers hear the roar of a tiger. There are rhinoceroses and elephants. In the flat areas of the Ganges River you could find the famous Bengal tiger.

Forest

The **forest** areas are filled with leopards, wild boar, deer and birds. Peacocks and parrots are the most colorful; the cuckoo and mynah are the chief singers. The elephants are also important here as "beasts of burden."

# of INDIA

India has hundreds of varieties of reptiles. The king cobra is the most dreaded. Along **jungle** trails are huge pythons which can swallow a small goat.

Jungle

Desert

In the **deserts** the camel is the main transportation. Camel carts are often seen in the desert cities.

Pretend you are assigned to draw and write a travelogue for a group of zoologists. They study animals. "Snap" pictures and write short information paragraphs to encourage the zoologists to visit India.

Hinduism

One of the most important things in the lives of the Indians is their religion. About 85 percent of the people are Hindus. About 10 percent of the people are Muslims. Christians are 2 percent and the rest are Buddhists, Sikhs (seeks), or Jews. Color the circle graph showing the religions: Hindus, blue; Muslims, red; Christians, green; other, yellow.

When Hinduism first began about 1500 B.C., there were beliefs in many gods of nature such as thunder, lightning, rain, sun and the moon. Later Hindu beliefs were written down into four statements: 1) a belief in God, 2) a belief in a soul, 3) a belief that man must be responsible for his actions, 4) a belief in reincarnation which means that people may live several lives.

One of the favorite folktales of the Hindus is told that Parvati asked her son Ganesh to keep everyone out of the house as she rested. Siva, Ganesh's father, returned home but could not get in. In his anger, he cut off Ganesh's head. His father and mother were very upset that their son was dead. Siva then promised to find a head of the first animal he encountered. It happened to be an elephant. When the head was placed on the boy's body, he came back to life and was then called Ganesh, the Protector.

The Indians enjoy reading their stories in comic book form. Can you draw a simple cartoon strip of this famous Indian folktale? Add "bubbles" for the words the characters speak.

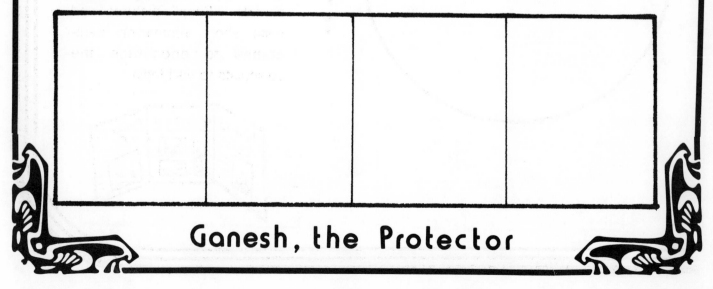

Ganesh, the Protector

FOODS OF FLAVOR

In a village home you will see very little furniture. There are usually no chairs or tables because people eat sitting on the floor. The pots and pans are generally made of clay, although metal pans are becoming popular.

The men are served dinner first and sit in a circle or semicircle on the floor. The food is eaten with their fingers.

A typical villager's meal would be unleavened bread, which is baked fresh for every meal; rice and curry powder; a vegetable; and red or green peppers for seasoning.

There may be some lamb, chicken or fish also served, if it's a special day. Also sweets are eaten for special treats.

The men prefer to drink tea and coffee.

A seasoning, called curry powder, is used often when cooking. It is a "zesty" seasoning made from these herbs and spices: ground mustard, coriander, chili powder, black pepper, ground cumin, fenugreek, ginger and garlic.

Herbs and spices all have different smells and flavors. Research some common and uncommon kinds of herbs and spices. Perhaps if each classmate brought a different one, you could try to guess the names and uses for each.

Herbs and Spices

SAMPLE

SPICE # ____

TRY TO MATCH

Name of Spice/Herb:

_____

Uses: _____

_____

From: _____

_____

There were once over five hundred Indian states and each was ruled by a maharaja. The maharajas became very wealthy over the years. They dressed in expensive clothing and wore glittering egg-sized jewels around their necks and on their fingers.

Since 1947 the maharajas do not have the power they had. They do still have their wealth.

In the city of Jaipur, you may see the maharajas and for special occasions you will see the royal elephants. These elephants are painted and jeweled. It may take as many as two days to elaborately decorate an elephant.

First, the elephant is painted with gold luck symbols. Toenails and eyes are painted. Special elephant jewelry is worn. This jewelry consists of heavy gold necklaces, silver coins on chains, enormous gold earrings and a large jeweled pendant for the elephant's forehead. Ankle bracelets with bells, golden tips for the tusks and brightly colored cloth for the back all represent the wealth of the maharaja.

Pachyderms on Parade

Decorate the royal elephant below. Work carefully so **you**, the maharaja, will be proud to ride on it!

ARTISTRY

Most women in India dress according to their religions. Some wear **saris** (SAH-rees) and some men wear Western-style clothes. The women's saris are in vivid colors and are handed down from mother to daughter. The saris with gold or silver embroidery are burned when they wear out. The metals remain while the cloth is the ashes. A sari is one long piece of material, 8 or 9 yards long, that is draped in a special way on the body.

The woman's fortune is also worn rather than placed in a bank. Bracelets, ankle bracelets and even nose rings are worn to enhance the woman's beauty.

Hindu men typically dress in white.

The Moslem women wear trousers and tunics. They also wear much jewelry.

Embroidery is a picture sewn on material with colored threads. Talented craftsmen embroider intricate pictures for shawls or rugs.

Try your artistic talent and "embroider" this picture or one of your own.

Cut out a 5" x 5" piece of paper. Glue onto cardboard. Draw a simple picture of India or use this picture. Outline with yarn and continue to fill in the area completely. When you're finished, no paper should show through. Frame with black paper.

CLOTHING

Long ago the Indian people were divided into four classes: priests, soldiers, merchants and peasants. Below these four classes were people with no caste. They became known as the "untouchables."

Today the government outlaws "untouchables" and the caste system. Informally, they still do exist and now instead of four classes, there are about 19,000 castes. According to Hindu religious beliefs, everyone is born into a particular caste and remains there the rest of his life. They also believe that everyone who dies is born again. If one dies free from sin, he will be born again into a higher caste.

TRY TO FIND OUT:

1. What jobs are done by people in the high caste?

_____

2. What jobs are done by people in the "untouchable" caste?

_____

3. What happens when people want to marry someone from another caste?

_____

4. What is done with the bodies of people from a high caste when they die?

_____

5. Do we have castes in the U.S.A.?

_____

6. Do you have castes in your school?

_____

The Ganges River is believed to have the power to wash away sins. The river is a famous river and has much significance for all Indians.

CASTES or CLASSES

GANDHI

Mahatma Gandhi (mah-HAHT-ma GAHN-dee) was one of the most important men who ever lived. He did not believe in the caste system that told people what jobs they would have and what lives they would lead. He devoted his entire life to helping poor people become free.

Gandhi was thinking of two kinds of freedom. One was the freedom of India. At that time, around 1914, India was being ruled by the British. The second freedom was from **prejudice** and **poverty**. Can you explain what you think these two words mean? _____

Gandhi did not use fighting to gain these two freedoms. He felt the best way to change bad laws was simply not to obey them.

The Indian people had lost their desire for simple crafts, such as weaving. In order to encourage the people to rely on themselves and not the British, he would do handweaving every day. He wanted the people to know there was no shame in doing handwork.

If you would like to learn to do finger weaving, the directions are below.

Materials needed: a small ball of yarn or string and 4 fingers!

Directions: Hold the end of the yarn in the palm of your left hand. Use your right hand to move the yarn around your fingers (in and out). Wind the yarn around your fingers again and now you have 2 strings facing you on the middle and pinkie fingers. Lift the bottom yarn over the top yarn. To continue, wind the yarn across only once. Take off yarn on fingers 1 and 3. Repeat this process until desired length. The knitted yarn will move down the back of the left hand. Ending: End with the ball of yarn on the left side near the thumb. Move pinkie yarn onto ring finger. Lift bottom over top. Move remaining yarn from ring to middle finger. Lift bottom off. Continue moving toward thumb. On last loop, cut yarn from ball and put end through loop. Pull tight.

Make a headband or belt for yourself. Add beads to the ends if you like.

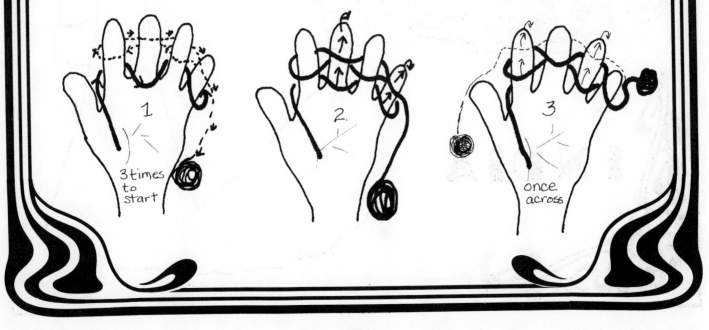

Color the costume on the left.

Design your own Indian costume on the right. Color carefully. Try the completed costume on the doll.

INDIA

Travelin' On ...

The following is a list of additional topics that interested or highly motivated students may want to learn more about:

Papier maché jewelry

Madras cloth

Indigo dyes

Buddhism

Ganges River

Indira Gandhi

Nehru

Wearing a sari

Cobra snakes

Sacred cows

Foods

Tulsi ("holy plant")

Family-arranged marriages

Movie industry

Sikhs

Muslims

Overpopulation

Relations with Pakistan

Kashmir

DEBRIEFING THE WORLD TRAVELER

An International Week would be a rewarding final activity. Each day a different country would be featured. A group of students would be in charge of the activities and portray the importance of their country to the rest of the class (or grade level, or school).

An International Game and Toy Show would be fun. Students could work in pairs to build a toy or game that is either authentic or uses information about their country. Each team could explain their game and then have others try it.

Creative dramatics in the form of student-made puppet shows would be enjoyable.

Shopping centers enjoy displays and programs, also. Cable television public service channels use school activities. This is your students' chance to become stars!

You Are Invited to an

International
TOY and GAME
Show

Date:

Time:

Place:

Use this invitation to invite other students or parents to your Toy and Game Show. Be sure the students are available to explain their toys or games to interested visitors. Prizes may be needed for visitors

who are winners. Small flags on toothpicks could be made for prizes. Each visitor is given a small ball of modeling clay in which to place the winning flags.

FOREIGN

Japan

VEGETABLE TEMPURA

Fresh vegetables cut into bite-sized pieces. Select any of the following vegetables: carrots, celery, eggplant, beans, mushrooms, squash, green pepper, cucumber, broccoli, cauliflower or parsley.

Dipping Sauce: 1 cup soy sauce or 1 cup Japanese **Dashi** (fish stock) boiled with ¼ cup soy sauce.

Tempura Batter:

2 eggs
1 cup ice water

¾ cup flour
vegetable oil for frying
(380 degrees)

Prepare the vegetables. Dip them into the ice-cold batter. Use vegetable tongs to drop several vegetable pieces into the hot oil. Fry for 1 or 2 minutes. Remove with tongs. Drain on paper toweling. Fry a few pieces at a time. Serve immediately with a small bowl of dipping sauce.

Peru

PORTUGUESE SWEET RICE (serves 6)

1 cup rice	salt	2 cups water
2 cups milk	1 tsp. vanilla	1 tsp. cinnamon
Thin slices of lemon rind	3 egg yolks	½ cup sugar

Cook rice in salted water for 15-20 minutes. Fluff rice with fork and let stand for 10 minutes. Combine milk, vanilla, cinnamon and lemon and simmer for 10 minutes. Let stand, off heat, for 10 minutes. Remove lemon rind. Cream egg yolks with sugar until pale yellow in color. Add the spiced milk. Pour into saucepan and stir over low heat until thickened. Add rice and continue stirring 2-3 minutes. Serve at room temperature with cinnamon sprinkled on top.

Quebec

PAIN PERDU (French Toast)

2 large eggs, separated	1/8 tsp. salt	½ cup milk
¼ tsp. vanilla	1/8 tsp. nutmeg	¼ lb. butter
2 tbsp. vegetable oil	6-8 slices French bread	
4 tbsp. sugar	jelly	

In bowl, beat egg whites and salt until stiff. Add yolks and continue beating while adding milk, vanilla and nutmeg. Mix well. Melt butter and oil in large skillet on medium heat. Dip bread into egg mixture to coat both sides. Place in skillet. Fry on both sides, turning only once. Remove from pan. Sprinkle sugar on one side and jam on the other. Serve at once.

FOOD FAIR

NORWEGIAN SUGAR KNUP

3 cups brown sugar   4 tbsp. water

In heavy frying pan, combine sugar and water. Bring to boil, stirring constantly with a wire whisk. Cook 2 minutes after a good boil starts. Pour into small pan. Score into small pieces at once. Break apart and store in tightly covered glass jar.

HERO SANDWICHES

1 Italian sandwich loaf or ½ loaf of Italian bread

4 lettuce leaves	2 tbsp. salad oil
1 tsp. vinegar	8 slices of salami
6 slices of tomato	6 slices of cheese such as provolone or mozzarella

Cut the bread in half lengthwise. Place washed lettuce leaves on bread. Sprinkle with oil and vinegar. Lay other ingredients on top in order. Cut into two sandwiches and serve.

GROUND NUT (PEANUT) CRUNCH (makes 15 1-inch balls)

¼ lb. unsalted peanuts	⅓ cup water
⅓ cup sugar	½ tsp. cinnamon

Shell peanuts and chop fine. In heavy saucepan, heat water and sugar over low heat, stirring constantly until sugar dissolves. Add peanuts and cinnamon and stir for 3 minutes until the sugar turns light brown. Be careful not to burn sugar. Remove from heat and cool about 10 minutes until cool enough to handle. Shape into 1-inch balls and place on waxed paper until hard.

FRUIT CURRY (serves 4 to 6)

2 onions	2 tomatoes	1 orange (peeled)
1 banana	1 green pepper	3 tbsp. butter
2 tbsp. sunflower seeds	¼ cup raisins	½ tsp. salt
		2 cups cooked rice

¼ tsp. curry powder or to taste

Peel, cut and chop onions, tomatoes, pepper, orange and banana. Melt butter in pan. Add onions and peppers and fry until soft. Add all ingredients except rice. Cook, stirring for 5 minutes. Stir in rice and simmer for 5 minutes, stirring constantly. Serve warm.

Norway

Italy

Kenya

India

GAMES

Japan

JAPANESE TAG

Materials: none

Directions: The one chosen to be "It" tries to tag a player. The tagged player must put one hand on the spot touched by "It." He must chase the other players with his hand in the tagged position. He can remove his hand from the spot only after tagging another player. Make the game more exciting and have several taggers.

Italy

FOLLOW THROUGH TAG

Materials: none

Directions: Players form a circle with their hands. They hold up their arms to make arches. One player, the runner, is inside the circle; the other player, the chaser, is outside the circle. The chaser tries to catch the runner but must follow the exact path the runner takes. When the chaser catches up, two more players are selected to be the runner and chaser.

Quebec

FRENCH BLINDMAN'S BLUFF

Materials: scarf

Directions: This game is played like "Blindman's Bluff" except that the person who is "It" has his hands tied behind his back instead of being blindfolded. This will help eliminate accidents and is a lot of fun!

India

SCORPION'S STING

Materials: none

Directions: Players gather closely around one player who is the scorpion. The scorpion walks on all fours and raises one leg to represent the stinger. The scorpion tries to touch another player with his stinger (raised leg). If he does, there is a new scorpion. The other players try to get as close as they can without getting stung!

GAMES

GAMES

AFRICAN GAME TRAP

Materials: March music

Directions: Play music for the players to march to. They form a circle. Two players form a bridge over them by holding hands. As the music plays, they move over the heads of the circle players. When the music stops, they "trap" a player inside. Players caught make more bridge "traps." Continue playing until all have been caught. Marchers sing or chant as they clap:

Lions and leopards, lions and leopards,
Hunting at night.
Lions and leopards, lions and leopards,
Catch the game!

FISHING GAME

Materials: 9-inch dowels   7" cords
              Hook and eye   corks or 1-inch dowels

Directions: Fishing poles are made from 9-inch dowels with a 7-inch cord tied to the end. At the end of the cord is a dressmaker's hook (hook and eye). The fish are corks or short pieces of 1" dowels that have a staple driven halfway into them. On the bottom of the fish is a number indicating how many pounds the fish is. Four players fish at one time. They try to catch the staples in the fish with the hooks on their fishing poles. When all fish have been caught, the total **number of pounds** is decided for each player. The biggest catch wins!

CALABAZA

Materials: Paper crosses or flat stones

Directions: This can be played by 4 or more. There should be one less cross or flat stone marker than there are players. Players form a circle and chant **Calabaza** eight times. **Calabaza** means "everyone to his house." After the eighth time, the players all run for a marker. The player without a marker is "It." "It" goes to other players and asks, "Are there any eggs?" The questioned player answers, "In the other corner." Meanwhile all of the other players are quickly changing places while "It" tries to get a place.

Kenya

Norway

Peru

GAMES

117

ANSWER KEY

Country: Japan, page 24
Title: Sports and Self-Defense

```
B C A E F H I O Z D Y M E A S T R
O M S R G B L I P A C H I N K O T
T E R O M N Y L A F G O E A I F S
G H T I V L F M N S W I M M I N G
S R I R V O L L E Y B A L L N O R
L E H B A S E B A L L C K E G Y O
W Y S O C C E R Y F O O T B A L L
C E L W I M K B L I N G T I S S O
T K E L N N M O V I E S I N N E T
V C O I L L G E Y G N I S S I N T
M O U N T A I N C L I M B I N G A
E H I G O N U Y L T S R D E O F V
F I S H B A S K E T B A L L F V I
N P U V E R S T A N R S V U N D N
R V I U Y O L M S E R L I E M O D
```

Country: Quebec, page 60
Title: Apples and Asbestos

```
    A G W I N E S A P
    J O N A T H A N  I J K L
  O M C I N T O S H  T U R T
  U S E N A M Y A T S A N C O
  G O L D E N D E L I C I O U S
  F S T N E R A P S N A R T A P
  G N O R T H E R N S P Y O E
  I N W G O S W E A L T H Y S
T W R O M E B E A U T Y E
  L I D E L I C I O U S
  C O R T L A N D T R
    A S G R I M E S
```

Country: Italy, page 69
Title: Volcanoes
a. Crater
b. Ash and lava
c. Lava beds
d. Conduit
e. Igneous rocks
f. Reservoir of hot magma

Country: Peru, page 84
Title: South America-Peru
1. Lima
2. Arequipa
3. Machu Picchu
4. Iquitos
5. Piura
6. Trujillo

Country: Peru, page 90
Title: Peruvian Parties

```
A I B G D N E K H L O V M O P
C O N J U N T O S Q T I R C S
T C U F V J W A O X I O Y E Z
I B G J C L H L D K N L E O F
A L L S O U L S D A Y I M B N
N O S P V U Z U T R A N W E X
E H Y A C Z D B G U I T A R C
U A E N C H R I S T M A S F F
Q R I G L P H M Z I N J O A R
K P E A S A N T D A Y S U I T
A V G W E I C X D A N T A R A
M H B J F Y N K Q Z R L O S P
```

Country: Peru, page 92
Title: Sierras

DOWN: 1. HUAYCOS   ACROSS: 2. PANCAKE
      2. PONCHO   5. CAMPESINOS
      3. CHULLO   6. SOROCHE
      4. FRIGID   7. SIERRAS

Country: Peru, page 93
Title: Coastline of Peru
1. Ocean seaports, Lima, petroleum, fishing
2. c. desert
3. Peru Current
4. It brings a rich source of food, anchovy
5. It is used as poultry food.
6. Answers will vary.

Country: India, page 98
Title: India
1. south
2. east
3. north
4. east
5. south